James Oswald Dykes

Plain Words On Great Themes

James Oswald Dykes

Plain Words On Great Themes

ISBN/EAN: 9783743339286

Manufactured in Europe, USA, Canada, Australia, Japa

Cover: Foto ©ninafisch / pixelio.de

Manufactured and distributed by brebook publishing software (www.brebook.com)

James Oswald Dykes

Plain Words On Great Themes

PLAIN WORDS ON GREAT THEMES

BY

J. OSWALD DYKES, M.A., D.D.

PRINCIPAL AND BARBOUR PROFESSOR IN THE THEOLOGICAL COLLEGE OF THE
PRESBYTERIAN CHURCH OF ENGLAND

LONDON
SAMPSON LOW, MARSTON & COMPANY
LIMITED
St Dunstan's House
FETTER LANE, FLEET STREET, E.C.
1892

PREFACE.

When I was invited to contribute to this series of "Preachers of the Age," my stated duty in the pulpit had come to a close through my appointment to a professorial chair. I accepted the invitation in the hope of finding a wider audience for words which I was no longer called on to address to a weekly congregation. It seemed, therefore, reasonable to make the little volume fairly representative of that variety in treatment, as well as in the topics treated, which every preacher aims at in his usual ministry. Hence the sermons selected are quite miscellaneous. They aim at no unity of subject and are arranged upon no plan.

A few of the number have, at one time or another, found their way into print, being "reported" for serial publications. All of them are given substantially, for the most part even verbally, as they were preached. I trust the "words" may be found as "plain" as the "themes" are "great."

If they afford to any reader a degree of pleasure at all equal to what the author had in preaching them, neither will have cause to be dissatisfied.

J. OSWALD DYKES.

38, Coolhurst Road,
    Crouch End, N.

CONTENTS.

SERMON I.
THE WISDOM OF GOD.

PAGE

"God Who created all things ; to the intent that now unto the principalities and the powers in the heavenly places might be made known through the Church the manifold wisdom of God, according to the eternal purpose which He purposed in Christ Jesus our Lord."—EPH. iii. 9, 10 (R.V.) 1

SERMON II.
THE ATTRACTION OF THE CRUCIFIED.

"I, if I be lifted up from the earth, will draw all men unto Me." —ST. JOHN xii. 32 15

SERMON III.
GLORYING IN THE CROSS.

"Far be it from me to glory, save in the cross of our Lord Jesus Christ, through which the world hath been crucified unto me, and I unto the world."—GAL. vi. 14 (R.V.) 29

SERMON IV.
OTHER-WORLDLINESS.

"The time is shortened, that henceforth both those that have wives may be as though they had none ; and those that weep, as though they wept not ; and those that rejoice, as though

they rejoiced not; and those that buy, as though they possessed not; and those that use the world, as not abusing it: for the fashion of this world passeth away."—I Cor. vii. 29-31 (R.V.)	43

SERMON V.
THE SON BROUGHT OUT OF EGYPT: A PARALLEL.

"Thou shalt also consider in thine heart, that, as a man chasteneth his son, so the Lord thy God chasteneth thee."—Deut. viii. 5. "When Israel was a child, then I loved him, and called My son out of Egypt. ... I taught Ephraim also to go, taking them by their arms; but they knew not that I healed them." —Hos. xi. 1-3. "She shall sing there, as in the days of her youth, and as in the day when she came up out of the land of Egypt."—Hos. ii. 15	57

SERMON VI.
GUARD THE DEPOSIT.

"O Timothy, guard that which is committed unto thee" (R.V.) (or in margin, "Guard the deposit").—I Tim. vi. 20 ...	73

SERMON VII.
LESSONS FROM JACOB'S DREAM.

"He dreamed, and behold a ladder set upon the earth, and the top of it reached to heaven: and behold the angels of God ascending and descending on it."—Gen. xxviii. 12 ...	87

SERMON VIII.
OUTSIDE A CLOSED DOOR.

"Behold, I stand at the door, and knock: if any man hear My voice, and open the door, I will come in to him, and will sup with him, and he with Me."—Rev. iii. 20	99

SERMON IX.
JESUS AND BARABBAS.

"Not this Man, but Barabbas."—St. John xviii. 40 "We have no king but Cæsar."—St. John xix. 15	113

SERMON X.
THE GENTLENESS OF CHRIST'S METHOD.

"He shall not strive, nor cry; neither shall any man hear His voice in the streets. A bruised reed shall He not break, and smoking flax shall He not quench."—ST. MATT. xii. 19, 20, quoting ISA. xlii. 2, 3 129

SERMON XI.
WATCHING BY THE CROSS.

"They sat and watched Him there."—ST. MATT. xxvii. 36 (R.V.) 143

SERMON XII.
UNTO ME.
A SERMON FOR HOSPITAL SUNDAY.

"The King shall answer and say unto them, Verily I say unto you, Inasmuch as ye have done it unto one of the least of these My brethren, ye have done it unto Me."—ST. MATT. xxv. 40 157

SERMON XIII.
THE TWO HALVES OF CHRISTENDOM.

"The kingdom of God is not meat and drink; but righteousness, and peace, and joy in the Holy Ghost. For he that in these things serveth Christ is acceptable to God, and approved of men."—ROM. xiv. 17, 18 171

SERMON XIV.
ROBBED OF ONE'S GODS.

"Ye have taken away my gods which I made ... and what have I more?"—JUDG. xviii. 24 185

SERMON XV.
LIFE IN ABUNDANCE.

"I am come that they might have life, and that they might have it more abundantly."—ST. JOHN x. 10 199

BIBLIOGRAPHY 213

THE WISDOM OF GOD.

SERMON I.

THE WISDOM OF GOD.

"God Who created all things; to the intent that now unto the principalities and the powers in the heavenly places might be made known through the Church the manifold wisdom of God, according to the eternal purpose which He purposed in Christ Jesus our Lord."—EPH. iii. 9, 10 (R.V.).

ST. PAUL'S thought in this passage is plainly this, that Christianity is the last and highest exhibition of the Divine Wisdom, with a view to which all things have been created.

Before we can hope to master such a thought, however, we need first of all to make it clear to ourselves what we understand by "wisdom." We do not call that man wise, however learned he may be, who in the business affairs of life acts like a fool. Nor are men of genius always counted wise, any more than men of erudition. We recognize, therefore, by our use of the term, that wisdom has to do with the direction of conduct. It implies the application of knowledge and intellect to some specific result. That is not all. It is not every sort of practical skill or sagacity which we dignify with this choice epithet—wise. It seems to me we reserve such praise for intelligence employed for the attainment of an end which is noble; good, that is to say, and also important. Suppose a man to apply his mind to an object which is either petty or base—as, for example, a trick to gain a private advantage—

we should call him cunning only, not wise. This is a kind of intellectual effort in which even the beasts of high organization can compete with us. It is essentially a savage quality. Or if a clever man lays a deep scheme to attain a certain political end for his party—an end that is morally colourless or of no particular value to the commonwealth—you give him praise for shrewdness and sagacity, but scarcely for wisdom. In short, you keep this noble word for a noble use. It denotes high intelligence consecrated to moral ends, selecting fit measures and combining and adapting them, so as to compass an object which is wholly worthy, elevated, and beneficent. In proportion to the grandeur and goodness of the end sought, on the one hand, and to the consummate fitness of the means employed, on the other, do we commend the wisdom of the wise.

Now, when we ascribe this attribute to God, as the Almighty Designer and Disposer of all things, what we ought to mean can be no less than this—that the Most High has a purpose in each thing He does; that His purpose is so excellent as to be worthy of Himself; and that He makes for it through methods than which none could be more fitting. So much at least we must believe concerning every separate act or work or arrangement of the Only Wise God. But although the wisdom of God can cover no less than this, it may be supposed to cover a great deal more. To be perfect, it is not enough for wisdom to design well each part; it should combine the parts into one whole. Even a man's wisdom is shown not so much in single trifling schemes for a small or passing result, as rather in his pursuing throughout life one supreme aim, grand enough to dignify all his endeavour. The more completely any one can keep such an aim steadily in view, binding his whole energy to the successful accomplishment of it, wasting no pains, but intending ever the highest results, the more surely does he deserve our praise for his wisdom. If we dare to compare small things with the greatest, can it be otherwise with the Infinite Intelligence which rules over all? Must not the perfection of wisdom be that He Who made and guides this wondrous whole has set before Himself through all its multiplicity one supreme and moral end to which everything tends; one aim, the best which perfect goodness can desire, pursued with perfect skill; one aim great enough to combine together all events as the steps which lead to its attainment, and good enough to repay the pains of so long a process?

This is certainly the loftiest conception of the wisdom of God to which natural reason can conduct us. I believe that Scripture lends sanction to it. Nay, more; I think that Scripture gives us certain hints by which we may guess how such a divine end or goal is to be attained. It indicates to us that every work of God known to us contributes towards one final purpose; and it indicates to some extent what that purpose is. We have been accustomed to classify the divine acts, so far as we know them, into three large groups, under the names of "Creation," "Providence," and "Redemption." The grouping is convenient, if only approximately accurate. At the same time, we must take care not to separate too much these regions of divine activity, as though they stood quite apart, or did not link into one other, or were not combined under any higher unity. That is not so. God's wisdom appears, indeed, in each of the three. In Creation: "The Lord by wisdom hath founded the earth." In His Providence: He makes "all things work together for good." In Redemption:

since it is above all by the Church that there has been "made known the manifold wisdom of God."[1] But far more than in any one of them does the adorable and consummate wisdom of Him Who is the Author of them shine forth in this, that He has kept one end in view through them all, combining Creation, Providence, and Redemption into the service of a single design. These three are but lower and higher stages in one and the same edifice; nor can we expect to understand even the lowest until we know what "far-off divine event" is by-and-by to crown the topmost of them with its glory.

My object, then, is to suggest to you this stupendous thought, that from the earliest dawn of the creation of our globe, right on through all man's history to its far-off close, the Almighty and All-wise God has been pursuing one consistent plan to one splendid, worthy issue. In that plan St. Paul teaches us that Christ's Redemption is the last and greatest factor; of that plan your salvation is the supreme issue.

The wisdom of God has been more commonly remarked and studied in the works of nature than either in providence or in redemption. But this is really because, of the three, nature is the lowest range, on which the other two are reared; in which, therefore, the exercise of divine wisdom is more simple, and more readily traced. When physical causes are combined with the skill of a contriver to attain some obvious mechanical or other physical result, any one can discern the purpose and appreciate the intelligence of so simple an operation. In proportion as the Great Worker

---

[1] Compare these texts: Prov. iii. 19; Jer. x. 12 (li. 15); Ps. civ. 24; Rom. viii. 28; Eph. iii. 10.

is dealing with material factors, while His moral aim is still remote or out of sight, in that degree are the problems those of pure intellect. For instance, nothing impresses the student with more wonder than when the formation and maintenance of the solar system can be referred to the operation of a very few majestic laws of motion, capable of being thoroughly comprehended and even expressed in absolutely correct mathematical formulæ. Here we are dealing with the simplest problems—those of dead, unorganized matter. The laws of animal life on our own globe are found to be much more complex. The laws of life, I say, not merely of organism. So long as we only study the Creator's wisdom in structural adaptations (like the Bridgewater Treatise writers in the early part of this century), the proofs of contrivance at least are easy. But contrivance is a humble description of wisdom. The real problems of biology are both more recent and more difficult. We are only beginning to discover how life has been generated, developed, and varied from age to age of a dateless past. Here, too, moral elements begin to enter—the happiness or suffering of sentient beings, the care which a good God must take for the least, the sacrifice at the same time of lower to higher forms of existence. Already, therefore, it has become a perplexing problem to say what end worthy of perfect wisdom can have presided over that long story of the appearance and disappearance of animated races, over that fierce and ceaseless struggle for survival, over the steps by which life strode to its maturer triumphs across the graves of a myriad tribes, that perished in the process. To justify this portion of the Almighty's plan is, perhaps, not yet possible until our science shall be more complete. It certainly is not likely that it ever can be justified until we see what all this was destined to lead to. With what interest, worthy of a wise Maker, has this globe been conducted through its past history of secular change, its materials built slowly up through the lives and deaths of unnumbered living creatures, and its features carved by the fires and frost of unknown millenniums? Can science tell? Or can piety, unless it keep in view the far loftier moral history of which the globe was destined to be the stage? In short, to discover a wise purpose in nature and its past evolution, you must ascend to man and to the moral providence of which he has been the subject. For the successive stages of divine activity do not carry each of them its own justification, because they do not exhaust each within itself its own meaning. On the contrary, they are linked to one another as the stages of a single plan, the parcels of one whole. Like the moves in a game, each prepares for the next to follow, nor can anything be explained to satisfaction till the end of all things shall appear.

Similar remarks will apply to God's providence in the history of our race. Neither can its end be seen, nor the wisdom justified which has presided over it, so long as you look at it apart from redemption in Christ. Here, in the moral history of mankind, a problem is offered to us too difficult and complicated for us to unravel. Why was the bulk of mankind left without a revelation from Heaven through twenty centuries, that it might be reserved for one small tribe? Why have huge areas of the globe been the home of only savage life, abandoned to races which either never emerged out of barbarism at all, or have long since relapsed into it? Why, when some nobler stock did struggle up into civilization, has a deluge of savagery been suffered to sweep over it again and again, throwing the world back to begin afresh? Why have war and slavery and superstition and tyranny doomed multitudes of human beings to hopeless misery? How shall we explain the rise and decay of nations, or the preventible waste of human life, or the frightful cost of suffering to the toiling masses at which civilization wins its showy triumphs? Can a thoughtful man, looking merely at the outward history of our race, and contemplating facts like these, pretend to discern running through it any wise and adequate purpose, worthy of Him Who is our Father in heaven? Cut off from Christianity, as a divine interposition to save, I confess that the philosophy of history reads to me like a doctrine of despair. I am not able to see, if you forget Christ's cross, that the human family is advancing towards any millennium worth the agonies of its past. History without Christ offers us an enigma with no key: a question without an answer. Just as physical nature demands man for its head, so does man's history demand redemption for its solution.

This is an aspect of the gospel which is made especially prominent in the writings of St. Paul. That comprehensive thinker was enlightened to see that the late appearance of a Divine Person on the stage of this world, for purposes of redemption and salvation, was a fact of capital importance for the understanding of God's whole counsel in the past, as well as in the future. In it he found a key to the puzzle. With a view to that event, he conceived that the long past, both of Jew and Gentile, had been planned in the unsearchable wisdom of God. He believed that the consummation towards which events were tending would be found, when this chequered story should have run out its course, to lie in the gathering up of all things into Christ as the Head of a regenerated humanity, and the subjection of a redeemed universe to the final reign of God the Father of all.

I do not affirm that the plan of God in the history of the past becomes wholly luminous or intelligible, even when it is read in this light of Christianity. One obvious reason for that is that we stand only in the middle of the process, beholding unfinished work. We are still a long way indeed from seeing the end-result attained. We have not even reached any clear conception of what that result is to be. The acutest Christian thinker, not less than the Christian child, has still to take the divine purpose very much on trust. Yet the gospel does cast a certain light upon the mystery, for all that. It makes it quite certain at least that a purpose there is, and a great one. Say that this world was built up, and man placed on it, and all the ages of sin and suffering endured, with a view to so pregnant an event as the incarnation of a Divine Person, and at once I can well believe that a plan worthy of God must run through the whole to dignify and explain it. Tell me that from the first God cared enough for His human child to propose to Himself this magnificent intervention in His own Person to right the wrong and heal the sorrow and reunite the race unto Himself in love; you make it probable in a moment that human affairs are no such tangled skein of confusion as they appear to be, but are being woven by All-seeing Wisdom into one web, in whose final pattern all the parts shall at last be found inwoven. The very fact that the Eternal has allied Himself in a mysterious fashion with this unhappy race of ours, has struck in at a critical and foreseen moment to be a Personal Actor in the human drama, has expended on the cross the whole treasure of

His own love and sorrow for some end connected with men's future happiness,—this means that God has made Himself responsible for conducting the destinies of humanity under its new-found Head to a suitable conclusion. I say, this forbids pessimism or despair. This justifies confidence and hope. This reconciles us to wait till we see the close. This prepares us for an end-result hereafter to be disclosed, noble enough to "make known to principalities and powers of heaven the manifold wisdom of God."

To be sure, we do not discern the concurrence of every part. We cannot trace the long process through and through: creation preparing the earth for man and his moral history; then the providence of history crowned at length by supernatural interposition; and at last the epoch of Christian civilization running out as it is going to do in a reconstructed earth. The scheme is enormously too vast for us to read it. Its innumerable factors lie far apart. Much must remain inexplicable, to keep us humble and test our trust in God. That is so: and that, too, is right. But enough is known, when we view it from beside the cross of our Redeemer, to assure us that the Lord God reigns; enough to bid us give thanks that His reign is love and mercy as well as justice; enough to make us quiet and still amid the perplexities of time; enough to show how minute and accurate and mighty is the overruling care of our Heavenly Father; enough to render thoroughly credible St. Paul's assertion that God created all things by Christ with a view to demonstrate through the Church His manifold wisdom; enough to extort from devout hearts even now the adoring doxology which shall peal with a fuller note when we learn all: "*To God the Only Wise be glory through Jesus Christ for ever. Amen.*"

From this scriptural teaching that God is conducting the world with consummate wisdom towards one blessed and beneficent result, many lessons emerge. I shall name but two ere I conclude.

1. Hardly any truth is better fitted than this one to calm the fever of uncertainty and dissatisfaction which at present possesses so many of the most active minds of our time. I have hinted already how the modern school of scientific and historical investigation has made it harder than our fathers found it to say, "Here we plainly trace the wisdom of the Almighty!" With the advancement of science I dare say the answer will be furnished to many a question which infant science has only been able to start. But, at present, problems emerge of which the solution is not yet to hand. Not only so. Men's minds are at present intensely occupied with social difficulties, and a great many people grow more and more dissatisfied with our existing Christian civilization. Things are not as they ought to be. A stir of change is in the air. Some are filled with hope and some with fear. What the upshot is to be, no man foresees. Meanwhile, multitudes are trembling for the future; and many more are ready to despair, as if a wholesome, regenerated, and happy earth were a dream never to be realized. Now, the words of our Lord Jesus seem spoken for such a time as this: "In your patience ye shall win your lives."[1] He who firmly trusts that Jesus is on the throne for the express purpose of guiding this misguided race to a glorious issue, and that all things in heaven and earth have been arranged to conspire together for an end worthy of the wisdom and love of God, he has learnt the secret of confidence and quietness. Change

[1] Luke xxi. 19 (R.V., margin).

under the rule of Christ must on the whole mean advance. We are involved in the stress and strain of a social revolution; but these are only travail-pains of the new humanity which is to be born. The nearer the ages approach to the consummation of all the ages, the intenser grow those spasms of human desire and effort after the grand event of time. Be of good cheer: "It doth not yet appear what we shall be." "But the end of all things is at hand."

2. Nor is the same great thought of less value to each of us in view of our individual fate. Providence may often seem contrary to our welfare because it is contrary to our wishes. Our way is in the dark; its issues are unknown; and full oft, when gloom as of midnight seems to settle down upon our private prospects, we are ready to question if really Wisdom does hold the helm, or at least if we are not being sacrificed to the larger interests of society. What can be more disheartening than for a man to feel that he is like a chip or straw caught in some tumultuous torrent, which whirls him along with it, irresistible, heedless of his fate; while it rages onwards, the mighty world-stream—whitherward? We *are* caught in a stream, but all its currents are under control, and it flows obedient to the almighty Will, led by infinite Wisdom, to an end of perfect Love. The great world-plan of God includes our tiny lives. We are not forgotten. We are not going to be sacrificed to the whole. Rather, all things are for us, if we are Christ's; since nature and providence are both handmaids to redemption; and we, the redeemed of the Lord, are His peculiar care, to the car of whose salvation the heavens and the earth are yoked. Let us trust and wait. God's way with the big world, and with our little selves, may baffle expectation. It may disappoint and perplex the wisest.

But all is in safe hands. One reigns Who is the Wisdom of God as well as the Brother of man: reigns, and fulfils all His pleasure. Patience, my soul: all shall be well!

"Well," at all events, for him who links his personal destinies to the Saviour of mankind! For it is perfectly clear that, if God Himself subordinates His age-long plans in creation and in history to the supreme aim of man's redemption, and is keeping that in view in everything, and has for that end laid all things into the hands of Jesus Christ, the Son of man, then here is the one secure spot to which each soul of us must make speed to anchor himself for time and for eternity—to Jesus Christ. Cling to the Cross and Person of the crucified Son of God, for He is the Centre of history and the Lord of the future. Subordinate your private ends to His ends. In all you endeavour or achieve, keep steadily in view the supreme purpose of God Most High, which is the redemption of men from evil. Make the temporal serve the spiritual, even as God Himself does. Let His aim be your aim—to work towards a kingdom on earth of justice, peace, and charity. Then will you be safe, because you will be on the winning side; swimming against the stream of society, indeed, but with the stream of divine tendency, and in the main current of the divine purpose. This is to be truly wise. Wise, as a creature can be, with a borrowed light; for he is but a fool who is not taught of God; nor is that to be called wisdom in man which has not been lit (as one lights a taper) from the sole sun of the Wisdom of God.

THE ATTRACTION OF THE CRUCIFIED.

SERMON II.

THE ATTRACTION OF THE CRUCIFIED.

"I, if I be lifted up from the earth, will draw all men unto Me."—
St. John xii. 32.

Could we forget for an instant the divine dignity of this Speaker, which sets His words above comparison with those of other men, we might class our text with the greatest of those famous sayings which have sometimes escaped the lips of great men at supreme moments in their career. It betrays the true heroic temper. It breathes the courage of a strong soul under apparent defeat; for it wrests victory out of the hands of disaster, and dares to predict success in the moment of overthrow.

Such sayings, when they are acts of faith, become prophecies. Any vain-glorious fool who trusts in himself may feel confident that he shall win in the long run; and his brag will be no prediction. But the hero of a sacred cause rests himself upon God. Then his faith, built on the eternal, carries a sure presage of future triumph. Even a wise onlooker in our Lord's day might have argued, "Such a life as this Jesus of Nazareth is leading cannot prove a failure, if God be God;" and he would have argued well. To Jesus Himself the same conviction probably came, not as an argument, but as an intuition. The certainty which possessed Him that He bore a mission from the Father and was about the Father's work, became in His soul a pledge that in the end He should draw all men to Himself.

Certainly the event has justified His confidence. So soon as He had died and risen again He began to be the foremost spiritual power in the world. Who, if not He, has exercised the strongest and most growing influence throughout modern history? Nay, what makes history modern, the old order changing to a new, but just this, that the Christ is in it? Long the central Figure in Christendom, He begins in our century to draw towards Him at length the remoter East and South. Amid the confusion of opinion which marks a century of change, the most fascinating question, dominating every other, remains this old one: "What think ye of Christ?" Some believe, and some disbelieve; at all events, this Jew Who was lifted upon a cross draws. Intellects He draws, if not always hearts; curiosity, where no faith; hatred, it may be, as well as love. But He draws all men to Himself.

More than this, and stranger than this, it is by His cross He draws. John understood His Master to select this phrase, "If I be lifted up," in allusion to the mode of death by which He was to die. More than that may lie in the obscure expression; for there is reason to think that to our Lord's mind death appeared but as the gate or preliminary step to His exaltation. But whatever else it may hint at, there is no doubt the phrase was at least suggested by the elevation of a sufferer upon a cross or gibbet. It points, therefore, to what was to be the last worst token of His utter rejection and defeat; to the extinction, as was supposed, of His too daring claims to Messiahship by a shameful despatch out of the world He had aspired to save.

Was He mistaken when He said that a cruel death by

crucifixion should prove to be the very instrument, or condition, of His power? On the contrary, nothing strikes a thoughtful student of Christianity and of its influence more than this—how much it has owed to its Founder's death. The first and, in some respects, the greatest of its propagandists understood this well when he said, "God forbid that I should boast, save in the cross!" It was a true impulse which led Constantine to plant the cross on the imperial standard as the symbol of Christian power. If we mean by the cross the facts and teaching which cluster around the death of Christ as a supreme display of God's holy love and a final satisfaction for human sin, then the cross lies in the heart of the Christian religion as the very secret of its strength. From the vaulted apse of the basilica since the sixth or seventh century, the Figure which has looked solemnly down on the worshippers from its golden ground has been that of the robed and regnant Christ, seated for benediction or for judgment on the throne of the New Jerusalem. And rightly enough; since beyond doubt our Lord's uplifting does include His exaltation to the right hand of majesty and dominion. It is the Pontiff Christ, High Priest and King in one, at Whose feet we bow to kiss them in our homage, laving them with tears of penitence, and covering them with the murmur of our prayers. Thus is He present as often as we meet in solemn worship, and over us out of His golden heaven He bends for ever tender and awful eyes. These are the insignia of His power. But the secret of it, where is that? How comes He by His throne, from beneath which flow the four rivers of Paradise regained, the "streams which make glad the city of God"? Whence has He such virtue to draw sinful and thirsty souls to His feet? The Latin basilica will not teach you that, with its august Judge and its mystic city; but the Gothic cathedral will. For there, right in the centre where the great arches cross, there used to hang through many a century no jewelled Figure, draped and crowned on a regal seat of honour, but a naked bleeding Victim fastened to a stake. A painful, yet a blessed spectacle, repulsive to fastidious taste, but how dear to broken hearts! The mediæval Church has much to answer for, and it left behind it a fatal inheritance of superstition. Yet this truth God did surely teach His servants then, that it is the atoning, suffering Saviour Who alone can draw all men to Himself. By that truth the Church of the North conquered. It was the mysterious power of the cross which tamed the rude fierce youth of the Teutonic peoples. I welcome the lesson. I do not wish it to be taught to-day as it was taught then. We want no rood or crucifix set up here to symbolize for us the attraction of the Crucified; for, with the open gospel in our hand, we need none. But the Crucified we must still keep where mediæval piety placed Him, in the centre of our Churches, in the heart of our hearts. Nor must we be ashamed to proclaim that the very secret of the strength of our faith, the root and fountain of all its power to draw, to reconcile, to satisfy, to calm, to chasten or revive the souls of men, lies still where St. Paul found it, and Constantine, and Bernard, in the cross.

Can it be explained, then, this paradox of Christianity—how its strength grew out of its feebleness? Can we account for it, that by His death of shame, Jesus Christ attracts and rules the world?

I think we partly can. To see a little way at least into this secret, let us pursue a simple line of thought.

1. To start with, recollect how the attraction of Christ is a moral force, operating through the affections of men, not compelling them from without. He draws, not drives, His subjects. He reigns over hearts made willing. Now, it is a rule of universal observation that of all moral forces the most prevailing is that of unselfish affection. To be the object of another's toiling, suffering love, of love that is constrained by no claim on my part, and that stipulates for no reward, is to be drawn by an invisible attraction such as few hearts can withstand. If anything can move a man, that will. Holy love is in the moral sphere what gravitation is in the physical. It draws its object to itself as the sun draws its planets. It has virtue to charm the most rugged and subdue the most wilful. It establishes an empire of affection, like which there is no other empire upon earth. Instances of this attraction lie on every hand of us. It is of such stuff the ties of family life are spun. By such unselfish devotion parents win their influence over their children. By kind spontaneous service, rendered at personal cost in the hour of need, friend hooks to himself his friend with a clasp tougher than steel. The loyalty of a party to its chief or of an army to its commander is a cold and feeble sentiment, comparatively, until it has been warmed into enthusiasm by hardships gallantly sustained or labours successfully undertaken in the common cause. These are commonplaces of experience; only they assist us to appreciate that divine love of the Saviour which is no commonplace, but the highest instance of a universal law.

If the kindness which spontaneously serves and suffers for another is the chief moral force of attraction between persons, then we must expect it to reside supremely in the Supreme. God is the Sun in the moral system. It is He Who, as Centre, must bind into orderly movement around Himself all moral agents. And this must be the secret of His sway. Because He, far more than any other, loves with disinterested, uncalculating and ungrudging love; because He, beyond all others, devotes Himself to our welfare, without reserve no less than without constraint or reward—therefore is He able to enchain the hearts of His creatures and lead them captive in a leash of love. But we never knew it of Him before, nor dreamt there dwelt in the divine nature such capacity for sacrifice for love's sake, until we saw it in the cross of His Son. There it broke forth like an unlooked-for discovery. It took this world by surprise. May we conjecture that it took the moral universe by surprise? That Jesus is Very God, revealing by His generous Passion unto death for sinners the innermost heart of Godhead as self-surrendering holy love—this makes the cross the focus or burning-point of the divine power. He draws all men unto Himself.

It is characteristic of this species of power that it grows out of weakness. He who would win by affection must not command. He must serve. He must stoop. He must endure. Self-abnegation, self-surrender, is the very condition of his influence over others. For it is through meekness, patience, forgetfulness of self, and gentle ministries to the hostile or unworthy, that love betrays its divinely heroic temper, and establishes by degrees its hold over the heart it seeks. Therefore its symbol is the cross. He Who was lifted up on it, an unresisting Sufferer, hiding His strength under the infirmity of pain, hiding His pain, too, under the strength of patience—that silent Victim of wrong, content to be mishandled and misunderstood if only He might purchase life for His murderers: He hangs there the perfect Type of overcoming love. Out of weakness He grows strong.

Had this been nothing more than a man's love, it would have been acknowledged to be the ideal and perfect flower of love. Because it was that at least, it deserved to be something more: the expression in human act of a higher than human love, of the love of Him in Whose image our hearts were fashioned. Say that it is Very God Who loves in this wise; and you make God on the instant surpassingly lovable, clothed in the might of an infinite attractiveness. He draws men unto Himself.

2. Still, what has just been said is not enough. I must ask you to accompany me through a few more steps.

There is some reason, as I have hinted, to suppose that the cross is the ultimate disclosure of the self-sacrifice to which divine love can stoop, so that it has become a centre of attraction to others besides our own race. Scripture represents those pure intelligences who inhabit other regions of the universe as drawn to the uplifted Christ with a reverent interest, even curiosity, which is probably due to something else besides their sympathy with man. Around the cross they cluster, over it they bend, not for our sakes only but for their own. It has a fascination for them, we may humbly suppose, because it tells more than they knew before of the inexpressible tenderness and strength of His lovingkindness, Who is their God and Lord, the majestic Object of their devotion and the Centre of their affection. Therefore it attracts them also. It draws their admiration forth to the Deity; it draws their confidence; it draws their praise. If the suffering of the Son for a sinful creature has made God more lovely and adorable than any earlier manifestation of the Divine, then one can understand how the mean dishonoured stake on Golgotha may have become in sober fact the centre for ever of the moral creation.

Ah, had men only been as the angels are! How swiftly and how surely would He Who was lifted up have congregated all of us around Himself! But what draws the pure to God does not of necessity attract the criminal and the bad. On the contrary, this power which resides in holy love tells most upon the best. Pure hearts behold the beauty of God. Fearless, because stainless, consciences respond with promptitude to the call of noble love. Generous bosoms thrill to the generous deed. Does it follow that you can draw so easily mean natures that are polluted by impure passion or darkened by guilt and selfish apprehension? Must we not admit that the most divine of all conceivable actions may discover none of its loveliness to an evil mind? may fail to reconcile a rebellious will to the Divine Law, or pacify the alarm of an accusing conscience, or win back to God a hating heart? Though the nature of love is to attract, it does not follow that its attraction must succeed in overcoming either the repulsion of a wicked man or the cowardice of a condemned man. These are antipathies which have driven all of us more or less from God; and they are hard to neutralize. The task, therefore, which Jesus set Himself to solve was one of exceptional difficulty. Love's problem in our case was not how to fascinate the good, but how to reconcile the evil. To cure us sinners of the love of sin; to shame us out of self-will; to dissipate the prejudices and hush the fears of guilt; to make the Judge Himself attractive in the criminal's eyes:—this is the task of the Saviour's love.

It seems clear that no representation of the cross will

show how this task has been accomplished which stops short at a simple exhibition of the divine kindness. You praise God to me as One Who is so good that He will even die to show His love; and, if I were a good man, I should own such a Being at once and crown Him Lord of my heart. But, then, I am a bad man, not good; guilty as well as evil. I dread the displeasure of even so kind a God as this; and I have reason to dread it. I dislike His commandments, for they are at variance with what I naturally choose. Until you can do both these things, free me from His condemnation and reconcile me to His authority, I simply cannot love Him. Therefore you need to go further than you have yet done. Tell me, not merely how He loves well enough to die, but how His dying has cleared away the obstacles which close my heart against confidence and affection towards Him and His holy will. Make it plain to me that in His death He meant to make satisfaction for my crimes, so that He might be free to forgive and reconcile even me—the criminal and rebel. Show me the sin atoned for which I have done, and the wrath pacified which I have merited, and the holy Law of the Righteous One no longer armed against my life. Then I am able to open my heart without misgiving or distrust to the attraction of His love. Cancel the accusing past, and it will be possible for my suspicions to be disarmed, and my dislike of God to be removed. For then He is no longer a Being at war with my peace, the very thought of Whom stings me with reproachful recollection of an irretrievable past and apprehension of an evil future which I have deserved.

This is what the cross really does when we read it aright. It wipes out the past, not with a sponge of oblivion, which were no true relief, but with atoning blood by which the due of sin is owned and met. It stills, not overbears, the voice of conscience. It cancels our debt to heaven. It restores the soul to peace. It opens to the penitent the arms of divine favour. Only when its virtue to do this is apprehended, can the ineffable generosity which provides such a ransom for my guilty soul find unhindered access to my heart. Then, indeed, it conquers me. It sets before me a God not only lovable, but Whom I can find it in my heart to love. His goodness no longer alarms or condemns me. It only makes me ashamed of my alienation, and attracts me to its bosom. The Christ uplifted to redeem my soul from sin draws me to Himself.

Has it now grown in a measure intelligible why the power of Jesus to move the world turns upon His elevation on a cross? From the atoning purpose of His death for sin, and from its efficacy to reconcile us to God, springs every claim He wears to be the Friend of sinners, the Portion of the heart, or the Lord of the will. Already I have borrowed one illustration from mediæval art. Let me venture to borrow another. One of the noblest of the monuments which the Norman race has left in Northern Europe is the minster reared by William, greatest of the Norman name, to be the sleeping-place of his dust. Over the central portal of that ancient church, boldly carved within its arch to meet the eye of every entering worshipper, is a cross. Upon the four limbs of the cross you read four Latin words, each word reading inwards to the centre, and each of them terminating in the letter which forms a cross. The words are LUX, PAX, LEX, and REX. What is the meaning stamped there since the eleventh century, to be read so long as that abbey church shall stand, but this? If He Whom Christians worship be the Light of the world, and the Peace of the soul, and the new Law of liberty, and the King of loyal hearts, He has won each title by which He can draw men unto Himself from the cross on which He was lifted up.

This witness is true. Is Christ the Light of men? It is because by His cross He has revealed the light of that glory of God which is His self-offering love. Is He our Peace? By the blood of His cross He made our peace with God, so that there is no longer any condemnation. The new Law of Christian love—that ye bear one another's burden, and lay down your lives for the brethren —where does it find its illustration or its sanction but in the Master's own example? Our King is He, Whom we are to follow in uttermost loyalty? What is the crown we place upon the Saviour's brow when we enthrone Him in our affectionate devotion but a tribute of our gratitude to Him "Who loveth us, and loosed us from our sins by His blood; and He made us to be a kingdom, to be priests unto His God and Father. To Him be the glory and the dominion for ever and ever. Amen."

GLORYING IN THE CROSS.

SERMON III.

GLORYING IN THE CROSS.

"Far be it from me to glory, save in the cross of our Lord Jesus Christ, through which the world hath been crucified unto me, and I unto the world."—GAL. vi. 14 (R.V.).

LIKE every powerful thinker, endowed with marked individuality of intellect, the writer of this sentence has a singular way of expressing his ideas. He has forged a phraseology for himself. The thoughts, too, which he had to utter were strange and difficult. Language had to be compelled to a novel use. It is not without some trouble, therefore, that we can understand St. Paul. Nor can we be always sure that we have grasped the truth which struggles to the birth through his peculiar vocabulary and labouring metaphors.

However obscure these words of the text may be when you try to spell them out one by one, this much at least is clear. St. Paul means to say, very energetically, that, in consequence of the death of Christ, he and the world have no longer to do with one another. "The world and I," he virtually says, "have parted company; we are mutually dead to the influence of each other."

The difficulty here is to assure ourselves what he means by the term "world." "A man and his world" is a phrase which we understand pretty well. Every human being is environed by a set of surroundings which limit, and in part determine, his activity, but upon which, in his turn, he is able to operate, modifying them or making the best use of them he can. That complex of surroundings, or environing circumstances, make up the man's "world." It is the sum of things external to himself to which the man stands related. Assuming this to be the sense in which St. Paul employs the phrase, in what sense had he and his world cut connection? Clearly not by physical severance. To the world of natural fact, still more to the social human world of his contemporaries, St. Paul was by no means "dead" in any material sense; on the contrary, he continued to be a particularly energetic member of society, influencing the world in the middle of the first century very profoundly. The connection of which he is thinking, when he says here that it is severed, must be of a different sort. It can only refer to some sort of inward or moral connection with the world. He must mean that he has ceased to feel himself in moral sympathy or accord with his surroundings.

What this means we may be better able to see if we ask the question, When Paul and the world broke connection, what took the place of it in his life? If through the death of Christ such a change ensued that he ceased to be influenced by the world as formerly, what came to influence him instead? We shall get his own reply to this question, I think, if we compare a parallel passage in another of his letters, not remote from this one in date, where his phraseology strongly resembles that of our text. The Second Letter to Corinth has these words: "If any man is in Christ, he is a new creature [or, 'there is a new creation']: the old things are passed away; behold, they are become new."[1] This reads very like our text. Here also he goes on to say in the next verse that the only thing which now counts for anything is "a new creature." The "old things" now grown obsolete, of which he speaks to the Corinthians as things with which a Christian convert has nothing to do, must be just that "world" to which St. Paul tells the Galatians he himself is "dead." What, then, are the "new" things that have taken its place? This he proceeds in the Corinthian passage to explain, when he says, "All things are *of God*, Who reconciled us to Himself through Christ." From this explanation one may fairly conclude that in St. Paul's peculiar language "the world" and "God" are mutually exclusive terms. To be done with, or dead to the one, is to have to do henceforth with the other. The "world" which is grown obsolete, antiquated, or ineffective to the Christian, is a world without God; in other words, a man's present surroundings in this life, in so far as their moral influence has been irreligious or ungodly. The new universe into which his faith in Christ has introduced him is a universe of moral relationships and forces, which have God the Reconciler for their central Figure and ruling Force.

I think, then, we shall not greatly err if—to paraphrase the text—we say that the change wrought on Paul by the death of Christ was this: Previously he had been in sympathy or living intercourse with things in his surroundings which were irreligious or out of harmony with the Divine; whereas now such things have ceased to affect him as they did, and the only things he cares to live among or have commerce with are those which stand in ethical harmony with the will of God in Christ Jesus. The change, thorough

---

[1] 2 Cor. v. 17.

as it is, is not a change in his outward circumstances, but in the man himself. The world is what it was before. He moves about in it as he used to do. Only he is not the same man as he used to be, but morally and religiously an altered man. Therefore the world is not to him what it used to be, but morally and religiously an altered world. It is a graphic description, one perceives, for the greatest of all inward revolutions. A man who has been ungodly becomes godly, and instantly the world, in so far as it is without God, lying, as St. John says, "in the evil one," becomes inoperative, dead to him and he to it.

It is curious to notice what an exact contrast St. Paul's idea of life, as here pithily condensed, offers to that which, under the name of "secularism," is now so persistently recommended to modern society. The secularist and the apostle form as neat an antithesis to each other as you can desire. Of secularism the aim is to eliminate both from the world and from the soul every reference whatever to a Supernatural or Divine Being. "Get rid," it tells us, "of the conception of God altogether, and of everything which relates itself to that old-world conception. Then let a man reconcile himself with his material environment, so that man without God shall be really at home at last in a world without God. Then for the first time will this world, which knows no God, become everything to me, and I, knowing no God either, shall become really alive to this world, making the best I can of it." Such a theory of life, nakedly put, shocks you. Yet it is nothing but the formula which underlies practical irreligion. It is the only scheme of existence which can justify an ungodly life.

The ideal which St. Paul had framed for himself goes as far as it can go in the opposite direction. To him God is so near, so real, so supreme, so absorbing, that everything which is not God, or has nothing to do with Him, as good as vanishes from Paul's horizon. This very world itself is as nothing to him unless he can find God in it. Be it, as you say, a "godless" world—not in the secularist sense of a world empty of God, to be sure, rather brimful of Him— yet in its ethical spirit and conscious drift estranged from the Divine and out of sympathy with it: then, in so far as it is that, Paul is out of sympathy with it; must decline to yield it any place or influence in his life; must treat it as non-existent or dead. His true life he wraps up in God, and shuts out the godless world decisively.

To such an issue I venture to think it must come one day with each of us, and indeed with society. There are but two schemes of existence logically admissible: either Paul's, in which God is everything, or the secularist's, in which God is nothing. Which of them shall it be?

It may assist us a little to reach a more Paul-like attitude towards the Divine, if we can next discover how he reached it. How was it, does he tell us, that the unseen love and power of Him Who made the world had grown to be so engrossing a reality to this Jew—God the one living Force in his life, and he alive to nothing else but God? How came this about?

By "the cross of our Lord Jesus Christ," is his reply. But the meaning of that also is not at once clear. To comprehend this reply, let us try to see in what way the life and death of Jesus, as Paul understood them, altered the situation for him.

1. For one thing, they made the Divine Being very near and very real indeed.

One root of practical infidelity, that is, of the ungodly life, has certainly to be sought for in the invisibility of the Divine. Apparently, God is absent from our human world. He is inaccessible, at all events, to our human senses. We cannot find Him anywhere. Mankind before Christ went about, in Paul's phrase, "groping after" God, as one gropes in the dark for an object suspected to be there yet nowhere to be found. He was not far, to be sure, from any one of them. Yet they had to "seek God, if haply they might feel after Him, and find Him."[1] How could bad men be expected to care much for the presence of a Being of Whose very existence the best of men were not so very sure?

To St. Paul the appearance of Jesus Christ had changed all that. It set the Eternal Father in the most brilliant light as an actual Person. It brought Him into the closest and most certain relationship with every human being. It was the discovery of God once for all as a palpable, accessible Presence in our human world, never to be any more far off or questionable. To St. Paul, as to St. John, the Invisible had yielded up its secret. The Eternal Son, Who from the beginning had been the Image of the Father, had become veritable flesh in the Man Jesus, and was now one of us; so that henceforth, when you gazed into any human countenance, you could not forget that so God looked once while He dwelt on earth, or that still in His glory the Son of God is for ever such a Son of man. What a change this wrought! Instead of being a race without God in the world, left to grope helplessly after a hypothetical Deity, Who, if He existed at all, seemed to have forsaken them; lo, men have received God into the midst of them, and He

---

[1] Acts xvii. 27.

and every man who walks the earth are knit henceforth in a surprising kinship. Startlingly real is the Father Whom we behold in Christ! Awfully near to each of our souls!

2. Not only that, but the cross of Jesus discovered God to be a Person all compact of lovingkindness, especially of "philanthropy," or lovingkindness for mankind. This seemed a natural sequel to His union of mankind with Himself in the Person of His Son. For He surely could not be one of us without making common cause with all of us. Our interests became at once of necessity His interests. By the Incarnation has not God engaged Himself to further our welfare with all His divine resources? So that Christ is a personal link betwixt that sundered pair of contraries— Deity and Humanity; in Himself a gage of love, a league of peace: and His cross is the crown of His reuniting, reconciling work. In the cross St. Paul saw the spot where Heaven's mercy stooped to wed to itself Earth's guilt and misery. The blood shed for our redemption became the seal of a new-born alliance of man with God. What could that mean for our race but hope—illimitable, splendid hope of salvation? If the coming of Christ was not only an indubitable appearance of God within our horizon, but if He also came in the character of man's Reconciler and Deliverer, how must this fact have power to quench in its own light all meaner fires, and henceforth to burn within our hearts like a sun without a rival? Something like this must always be the effect of Christ crucified so soon as the religious significance of the cross is discerned. It is impossible to take in the love and help for our poor humanity which blaze out upon us from the death of God's own Son to redeem us, without owning that nothing else is comparable with that in its moral importance and transforming

power. By this cross of love dying to save, God sways back again to Himself the great ocean-tide of human affection till the opposite strand of secular ungodliness is left deserted and bare.

3. Especially does this result follow when, in the third place, a man feels how the cross has judged the world. I mean that, by the death of Christ for sin, the current opinion of the world concerning God has been corrected and its revolt against Him condemned. The chief charges to be laid against the attitude of average men towards God are, first, that in their ignorance of the true character of God they misrepresent Him to themselves; next, that in a mistaken desire for independence they resent His authority as an unreasonable restraint; and lastly, that they prefer to shake themselves rid as far as they can of whatever reminds them of Him or of His claims over their devotion. Now, the combined folly and criminality of all this do not become quite apparent until we read in the death of God's Son His real character and attitude toward us. It is there that the opened eye of the heart first learns that God is not eager to punish, but generous to atone; that His rule is not terrible as we supposed, but a rule of kindness; that to obey His law is liberty, not bondage—to disobey it not manly, but shameful and ungrateful; that our sins in the past offer no longer a hopeless bar to our return into His favour; that, on the contrary, He waits to receive and is prompt to forgive us for Jesus' sake. Our false judgments regarding God are corrected; our false excuses for ourselves are silenced. Instead of finding reasons for fleeing from God, or avoiding Him, or desiring if we could to blot Him from our thoughts, we see how monstrous has been the crime of such attempts in the past; how, on the contrary, our life must now lie in

being reconciled to His justice, forgiven by His mercy, and taken back into His grace. Once a man learns all this for himself, as he surely may learn it at the cross of Christ, the whole image which he had fashioned to himself under the name of God grows reversed. One becomes ashamed of the caricature of Deity which one had formed, and of the dislike and dread which that caricature called forth towards Him. The old bad reasons for leading an ungodly existence, as if one's world were most to one's liking when most empty of God, are gone for ever. A place where God is not, or where He can quite easily be ignored, is no longer the place for me. The centre of attraction for my whole nature is shifted. Rather I wish now to be where God is nearest to me—such a God as Jesus' cross discloses. To see His face, to feel His kindness, to draw inspiration from His Spirit, humbly to do His will, devotedly to advance His ends,—this has become all the world to me; and that old outside world of worldly men, where every one's ambition is to drown in business or in amusement the very thought of God, can be my true world no more. For all intents I am as good as dead to it. It is dead to me.

The revolution which St. Paul so energetically describes out of his private biography has thus to find its parallel in every thorough Christian. In your life, also, and in mine, the crucifixion of the Son of God for sin has to develop its inner meaning and force until we grow ashamed of our share in the world's ungodliness, and find ourselves set into fresh relations with God. This we may express in other ways than St. Paul's. Our phraseology may not be exactly his. Our experience of the altering power of the cross may come more gradually than his. It may be less revolutionary in appearance. Still in substance it will be the same. Every Christian is a man who is learning at the cross to find the glory of his life more and more in God, and not in that world which is at variance with God. Pray you, let your eyes open to the meaning of the cross, and surely your heart must burn beneath its heat of love. Surely the soul is so made by God that if He be beheld in His supreme revelation, as He truly is in Christ, He must sway its tides as the moon the ocean; He must draw me into an orbit of revolution as the sun the planets; He must become the Centre, the Sovereign, the Gladness, and the Pride of my life. This I take to be what St. Paul intends under that word he is so fond of, and which he uses in the text. Translate the Greek word how you please—to glory, or to boast, or to exult, or to triumph, or to rejoice—it must point to that which each man counts to be the highest and most worthy in all the circle of his life. That to the Christian can be nothing else but this—the revelation of God's redeeming love in Christ, of which the cross is the abiding symbol.

To understand, in conclusion, this Christian attitude of triumphant joy in the cross, let us seek to break it down a little into its components. So shall we be the better able to test ourselves by it in practice.

(*a*) Glorying in the cross involves that God in Christ is the sole basis of our religious confidence. This springs out of the context in which the text occurs. St. Paul is here waging war against ritualists and legalists; against men whose hope for eternity rested partly upon a minute compliance with ceremonial, and partly upon the blamelessness of their behaviour. But neither ritual nor righteousness can be an object of religious confidence to one who apprehends as St. Paul did the meaning of Christ's cross. Such recommendations cease to have any relevancy or value in procuring for a sinner the favour of Heaven, so soon as one perceives that, by the death of His Son, God designed to condemn sin and make atonement for it, so that He might be free to blot out transgression in His free and overflowing mercy. Atonement by the sorrow of God Himself, obliterating every sinful record and calling every son of man to the arms of divine favour,—this is for ever incompatible with a painful and punctilious religion, which toils to merit heaven by external rites and scrupulous legal observance. To glory in the cross must mean, at the least, to ground on it all one's hope of eternal life.

(*b*) It means more : that God is the Object of supreme desire as well as the ground of religious security. Out of everything which has not God in the heart of it or at the root of it, the charm is gone so soon as one's nature falls completely under the influence of the cross. After the objects of secular desire a worldly heart pants, not because in them it tastes something of Him Who is the Former and the Giver of them all, but for their own poor sakes alone. It pants after created Good because it has lost the Better—the Best of all—which is God Himself. That ceases by degrees when God begins to fling around the heart the net of His own love. Then that only will please which is His and is seen to be His; that which He made for us to enjoy and which comes to us from His hand; that in which the soul descries a little of His own goodness. Just in the proportion in which God is discerned in things desirable, are they to be desired by the perfect lover of God. It is a small matter to say that this robs impure pleasures of their fascination. It makes far better things than these seem poor and unattractive in comparison of holier joys. All things lovable it sorts after a new standard of value. Whatever fair or sweet things of the earth can be linked with His dear name Who is the soul's chief Good, especially whatever wins in Him the promise of an eternal worth, that borrows from the cross a tenderer grace and touches in the devout heart a holier joy. Thus it comes about that while on all things evil Christ's blood is set for a brand, that the soul may shrink from them in horror, on all things good it rests for a consecration, that the saints may find in them a keener, if a soberer, gladness.

(c) Perhaps it may signify yet more, this glorying in the cross. Meanwhile, God our Saviour is to be to us (would that He were!) the chief Object of desire, in Whom all other good and perfect things delight us. More and more must He not become to those who know Him the Satisfaction of desire and the Object of their proud possession? By-and-by, long after the possessions of the world have passed out of use or memory, shall not this sole treasure abide for the imperishable heritage of the saints—the love of Him Who died for love? When a day comes in which all that this world holds precious shall have lost its value, nothing will be left for any of us to be proud of save only this—that He is ours Who on the cross laid down His life to win us for His own. O ample revenue for eternal years! O proud soul that hath learned to glory in the cross of Christ!

OTHER-WORLDLINESS.

SERMON IV.

OTHER-WORLDLINESS.

"The time is shortened, that henceforth both those that have wives may be as though they had none; and those that weep, as though they wept not; and those that rejoice, as though they rejoiced not; and those that buy, as though they possessed not; and those that use the world, as not abusing it: for the fashion of this world passeth away."—
1 COR. vii. 29-31 (R.V.).

FEW careful readers of St. Paul fail to remark his habit of passing from a present instance to the wider principle involved in it. This habit of mind is well marked in his First Letter to Corinth; to it, indeed, the Letter owes its permanent utility for the Church of Christ. The difficulties on which he was consulted, for example, by Christian heads of families in Achaia, respecting the giving away of their marriageable daughters, have long since ceased to trouble. Even the peculiar "distress" then prevailing in the Roman empire, on which the apostle founded his recommendation of a single life, is a matter now of remote history. The world has lasted very much longer than St. Paul, I dare say, expected, and has changed so strangely in its "fashion," or the outward form of its civilization, that St. Paul, were he to come back, would not recognize it. But the incisive and powerful intellect of Christ's minister was enabled by the Holy Spirit to penetrate, beneath these passing occasions, to broad views of Christianity, and of the duties which it creates, and of the new relations which it has established. The principles which he was thus led to enunciate will never grow obsolete. These are as fresh and as true and as guiding for us to-day, as they were when Paul's new-writ roll of manuscript was first unsealed in the *salon* of Titus Justus, or wherever the Corinthian converts were in the habit of assembling.

Nevertheless, the ancient instance has left its imprint on the form of the apostle's teaching, so that we need to understand a little of that far-away time before we can fairly disentangle for ourselves the enduring lesson.

Paul was writing some two or three years after Nero became emperor, at a period which has been called "one of the worst epochs of ancient history." "Life," adds Renan, "seemed to have lost its motives; suicide became common."[1] The whole power of the world had got into the hands of "monsters and madmen." Immorality in the higher ranks was appalling. Prodigies and disasters awakened the gloomiest forebodings in superstitious minds. Even calm observers could see neither remedy nor end to the misery. Naturally enough, the Christian disciples, with their minds full of a splendid hope, read in these public evils and calamities so many signs of their Lord's immediate return. It was impossible for them or any one else to foresee the reaction in favour of better things which set in after another generation had passed away. Still less could they foresee that the empire would stand for centuries to come, or that, when it did fall, it would fall only in order that a new Christian world might be built upon its ruins. They simply lived at one of those dark moments which have now and then occurred, when the minds of men, unable to discern a glimmer of dawn on their horizon, abandon them-

---

[1] "Les Apôtres" (English translation, London, 1869, p. 260).

selves to despair, and think the day of doom must come to end the "distress." Another such moment arrived in the fifth century; another in the tenth. Society at times like these resembles a dying man. It really believes itself to be dying, and the voice of prudence to the dying is just that of St. Paul to Corinth: "Entangle yourself no more than you can help with fresh complications. Keep yourself free from distraction, that you may be ready for any change. The time is to be so contracted, that it is well to use the world as one who uses it not; for the fashion of it is shifting while we speak."

In the prevalent anticipations of his fellow-Christians on a subject regarding which our Lord says "no man knoweth," St. Paul possibly shared. But what was peculiar to him as an inspired apostle was this: He alone saw the divine intent in thus shortening to the eyes of that first generation their allotted season for earthly duty. If they were doomed to live beneath the overhanging pressure of such commotions and disorders as seemed to forebode the end of the world, this was designed to write deep on the Christian consciousness a great lesson. For thus the Revised Version quite accurately represents him as saying, "The time is shortened *in order that* henceforth Christians who weep may be as though they wept not," and so forth. That lesson, as we now know, was not to be for themselves alone, but for all Christians. In other words, out of that temporary pressure and expected curtailment of their own age there has grown up, in the divine wisdom of Providence, this permanent gain to Christian thought, this lesson for Christian life—that no Christian should abandon himself without limit to the interests or possessions of the present. Earthly enjoyments and sorrows are not to preoccupy or monopolize our minds, as though we had none other, none better or greater than they.

We are thus brought face to face with a mode of conceiving of this life which is due to the coming of Christ and therefore was quite novel when Paul was writing. To do it justice, one ought to realize for one's self how men must have felt who possessed no Christian revelation. Imagine, if you can, how one would live to whom this present scene was everything. With no living interest in any higher world than this, ignorant of what should happen to him after death, reduced to a dubious guess only whether there be any after-existence at all, is it not clear that a man in old pagan times had every reason in the world for throwing himself into present pursuits with a passionate and absorbing eagerness? To fill his heart and brain with secular affairs was all that was left to him. Therefore earth's joys possessed a relish, and were sought after with an avidity, such as we can scarcely conceive. When its losses came, too, its disappointments or disasters, the blow fell with a crushing weight, a sense of absolute and irretrievable loss, which to the Christian is happily unknown. Not that this state of mind is quite unknown to-day. It is the state of mind to which the materialism and secularism of our own age are driving not a few. For it must ever be a characteristic note of human thought and of human conduct in so far as these remain unchristian—this abandonment without reserve to the changeful passions of the hour; to life's mirth and life's desolation; to its chase after the intoxication of love or wine, after the gratification of ambition or of jealousy. Such abandonment all the philosophies of antiquity were powerless to moderate.

Not thus should the Christian live. To nothing earthly will he be able to give a place and power in his heart so unlimited as this. For him, too, as for other men, there comes the ambitious dream of youth, the sweet delirium of love, the felicity of home and children, the rewards of labour in prosperity, and the enviable honour that crowns old age. Yet in none of these good things will he suffer himself to rest as one who takes with no misgiving his fill of it. Never can he drain quite to the lees life's chalice of wine. No! nor its cup of wormwood either. The maddening sense of utter bereavement, of having nothing more left to hope for or to live for, which made suicide the recognized refuge of a brave Roman in misfortune, which yearly drives many of our own people to acts of despair,—that, too, is foreign to Christian experience. No loss of sublunary good can bulk in Christian eyes as it does, alas in those that have never been unsealed to behold the kingdom of God which endureth for evermore.

This is what I take St. Paul to mean when he bids us weep as though we wept not, and rejoice as though we rejoiced not. Indeed, he sums up his meaning in the significant formula: *Use this world as not using it to the full* (for so, with the margin of the Revised Translation, shall we best render it). And he clenches this rule with a reason which quite bears out our conception of it. "The fashion of this world," adds he, "is already changing." It is in the very act to undergo a transformation, as when you shift the scenery of a play; and therefore it is unreasonable to give your whole attention to the scene that is closing, and forget the one which is about to open. The metaphor suggested by his language is surely a most striking and significant one. We are living for a very brief space in the present scene of things, and here we have our part to play—our sevenfold part, as Shakespeare put it, should we live it out to the close. All the while there is another scene in course of preparation where we are likewise to be actors, and that right speedily; a scene which, once it is set up, shall not so quickly be dissolved. With that also in our thoughts, how can we give to passing events of to-day an undivided attention, or fill our hearts quite full with earth's passing goods?

I said that this sense of disengagedness, or (as old writers used to call it) of "sitting loose" to this world, was a novel consequence of Christ's teaching. Some of you may be tempted to think it is nothing else but the old idea, frequent enough in the Hebrew Scriptures and elsewhere, of man's life as a pilgrimage or at best a brief sojourn in a foreign land. No doubt it has a good deal in common with that. The Hebrews saw that life here meant only a "passing through" to something else, brief as the flight of birds, to quote the well known apologue preserved by the Venerable Bede; but they could not tell to what they were passing away. This only they knew, that they had found for their spirits a home in Jehovah, and Jehovah is everlasting; and so they trusted that, after this temporary resting-place knew them no more, He Who endureth for ever would still be somehow or somewhere a living Dwelling-place and Refuge for the souls that clave unto Him. It was a tender and wistful melancholy which stole over a godly Hebrew before Christ came, as often as he remembered that "we are strangers here," our "days on the earth like a shadow, and none abiding."[1] But the old feeling has changed its countenance now. Quite fresh thoughts have entered into

[1] 1 Chron. xxix. 15.

Christian experience. For one thing, we know where we are going. The home beyond has gained in distinctness since Jesus spoke of it. We have there on the other side, gone before us, our best and choicest Friend. That is true. But there is more than that. We have not to wait till death for a place in the eternal kingdom of God, or for a share in its eternal life. The kingdom of God is here. The life eternal has commenced. A Christian man has been already translated out of darkness into the kingdom of God's dear Son. He is a person, indeed, with two homes, situated in two realms; a citizen at once of two contrasted commonwealths. Even while we tarry among you here (may Christians say to the men of this world), and fill the offices of family men and subjects of the State, and do our best to play well our part in every capacity, being linked through God's ordinance to wife and child, to friend and neighbour, to society and the Church, by many a strong and gentle band, all the while, if we are Christian men, we do actually belong to the vaster company of the immortals. Our other citizenship is in heaven. Our truer home waits for us above. Our best affections are those that go up thither. It is a dual life we lead; and the longer we live it, the more do the earthly interests pale before the heavenly, so that as our time gets shortened we use this world more and more as though we used it not; because, consciously to ourselves, the scene is in act to shift and change. Almost while we speak to you these things of time are gone; lo! we are at home for ever with our Lord.

Do not be surprised, then, if your thorough Christian cannot let himself into secular affairs with the same undivided attachment to them which other men exhibit. There must be a touch of *other-worldliness* about him, an air of belonging to some far-off country. It is not an unwholesome sign if you detect this in yourself. It is not a thing you need wonder at in any other child of God. It has this for its inevitable consequence, that the Christian does not build here an abiding dwelling-place, or take too sorely to heart the buffets and vicissitudes of time. It would be extremely short-sighted in one who lives under the light which Christ's gospel has let in upon us, to suffer his thoughts to be fettered to things which are seen and temporal and transient, as though this life were all that it concerns a man to care for. No Christian can be so foolish. He knows that he has a building of God, eternal, in the heavens. Hence he forms no permanent plan, constructs no enduring house, on earth. Neither does joy engage his whole heart, nor sorrow. He is not so elated by a little success as if now he was to be happy for evermore; just as a new toy or game will make your child supremely blest—for half an hour. No; and when his dearest possessions wither at the touch of death, like flowers that blacken in an early frost, you will not hear him rend heaven or deafen earth with piteous passionate lamentation, as though everything had perished. After all, the loves and hates of earth are matters of an hour, so to speak. Its best joys and its worst sorrows form a mere fraction of the reasons why a Christian man grieves or is glad. Behind all these—behind home, behind business, behind fortune and fame, behind old age and the grave—the believing eye never ceases to behold one larger, grander, nobler good, standing there serene and shining like an Alp that stands for ever. It is the inheritance of God in Christ our Lord.

I do not know that there is anything about the experience of a genuine Christian, which is a greater puzzle to others, than this sense of belonging to another world more fully than to this one. One reason is that it does not work in Christian minds as unchristian observers expect it to do. People suppose it ought to make those who entertain it unpractical, unbusiness-like, or dreamy. It is expected that they will move through society with an indifferent air, like outsiders who have no business here and no interest in anything that goes on. Now, it does not act in this way at all. I do not mean by this that there are many so-called Christians who display quite an average concern about making money or attaining position in society, just as if they had their portion in this life. I am not thinking about inconsistent persons, who are at heart "men of the world" after all. No: but sincere Christians are just as active, diligent, and interested in life as their neighbours. They make to the full as good citizens. They do care about politics, and art, and education, and social reform. They toil as hard for their children, and they love their wives as well as other men do, if not better. True: there are certain departments of social life in which religious people cannot be got to show any interest. The world of sport, for example; the theatrical world, too, for the most part; the world of gaiety and fashion. But they are not alone in this. Others, too, limit their interests in a similar way. To make up for this abstention in some directions, are not religious persons exceptionally eager and occupied about other things? Modern Christians are not, and they do not profess to be, hermits retired from society; but plain everyday people, who carry on the business of their generation just like their neighbours. Seeing this, unchristian observers jump occasionally to the conclusion that the religious public is not sincere in its pretence of *other-worldliness*, but does really care for this world quite as much and quite in the same way as the rest of mankind.

The solution of this puzzle lies in two very simple considerations. For one thing, to belong to another world as well, does not prevent a Christian from belonging to this one in the mean time; and, in the next place, there are certain uses to which this world can be put, by way of preparation for the next, which compel him to take a great interest in it.

It is an obvious blunder to say, "I am not to play my part well where I am, because I expect the scene to shift, and shall presently have another part to play." The blunder, certainly, is one into which some fanatics at Thessalonica were betrayed through misapprehension of St. Paul's teaching; but they were promptly corrected by him. It is not the fair use of this world which is inconsistent with my relations to a higher one. It is only its over-use—its exclusive use—its monopolizing of me. I cannot let myself become, body and soul, the devotee or slave of any earthly person or thing, as though I had nothing beyond to live for. I cannot lavish my whole love on you, or become so wrapt up in anything that I am not prepared to part with it. But that is a very different thing from saying, I am not to love you at all, nor care for anything that happens, nor receive pleasure and pain, like my neighbours.

Nay, more: there are certain aspects of this life which start out into fresh urgency so soon as you tell me that I belong to the super-earthly kingdom of God. In fact, *all duty* acquires a new value under that light from the other side. For the Judge is standing behind the door. A moment more, and the folding gates may fly open at His word, so that I shall have to give in my stewardship. In that long Hereafter, which is for me the real world, my position is to be determined by my discharge of obligation here and now. It may have become to me a matter of less consequence whether I am happy now or unhappy—the time for that is so short; but it has come to be of far greater consequence whether I behave well or ill, for on that depends my happiness or unhappiness for evermore. The moral worth of actions is thrown into vivid relief by my faith in God and His kingdom. This lends weight to every action, and binds me to diligent and scrupulous discharge of obligations, even in the most trifling affairs. So that in one sense the importance of this world is actually heightened. It is a more serious world to live in than ever before, since now it is regarded as the moral preparation for a greater one.

In another way, also, this tells in favour of diligence and attention to secular concerns—tells against indifference or indolence. By making a just use of the present and of his opportunities in it, the Christian can amass enduring capital for the next world. Life, its powers, its chances, its responsibilities, are so much raw material in our hands. Well employed, they are to yield permanent returns in that life beyond. He, therefore, who works hard to make the most in a Christian sense of the present life, he is the Christian who will enter heaven the best furnished for his future existence. This is perhaps a thought not so familiar to our minds as it ought to be, often as it is taught by our Lord. Out of a charitable employment of money, He tells us, we may procure for ourselves everlasting friendships after death. It is in our power, He says, to lay up treasures that will not rust, and when we die to be rich toward God.

This is only to be done by making the utmost of each earthly talent or opportunity of service and usefulness upon earth, as good stewards of God's manifold favours. It is clear, then, that to fold one's hands and dream of heaven is the way to make one's heaven (when one gets there) a poorer place. Whereas now is each servant's chance to transmute the petty advantages and responsibilities of time into a future reward immeasurably higher.

See what a counteractive is here against indolence! The Christian a man who has little to care for on earth! Why, if he had nothing else to do with it, is it not at least his labour-field, where his diligence must be tested in the Lord's service, out of which, when the Lord comes, he has to reap the golden fruitage of his toil in the honours and rewards of a better life? The bands of Christian workers whom you behold hard at work to make this world better, are doing it for the good of their fellow-men in the first place, because the spirit of their Master is in them. But they are also doing it to their own infinite and everlasting gain, although they may not think so much about that. And while they keep their deepest affections aloof from earth and free for heaven, yet their hands are no whit less busy on that account—rather, all the busier and more unwearied, because "the time is short," and already "the fashion of this world is passing away." Up, my brethren! let us join them. So let us occupy till He come! With no abiding city here, but doing good as we have opportunity, because so swiftly the night will close our day of labour, and with the night comes rest; and with rest, reward; and with reward, the joy that is unspeakable and full of glory!

THE SON BROUGHT OUT OF EGYPT: A PARALLEL.

SERMON V.

THE SON BROUGHT OUT OF EGYPT: A PARALLEL.

"Thou shalt also consider in thine heart, that, as a man chasteneth his son, so the Lord thy God chasteneth thee."—DEUT. viii. 5.

"When Israel was a child, then I loved him, and called My son out of Egypt. . . . I taught Ephraim also to go, taking them by their arms; but they knew not that I healed them."—HOS. xi. 1-3.

"She shall sing there, as in the days of her youth, and as in the day when she came up out of the land of Egypt."—HOS. ii. 15.

IN view of such passages as these, is it merely fanciful to trace a parallel betwixt the history of God's ancient people and the course of a single life, as it passes through one stage after another from infancy to age? Are we not justified in saying that Israel the nation had, like us, its childhood, youth, and maturity? That God's way with it was the way of a father with his son, adapting His methods to its successive periods of growth, and through every vicissitude exhibiting the skill of an Educator with the unwearied, patient love of a Parent? If this be so, ought not such a reading of the Old Testament to be both encouraging and instructive to ourselves? I am about to attempt the working out of this parallel, at least in outline. I propose to show you, if I can, how Israel passed through periods which, to some extent, ran alongside the development of each man's individual life, and how Jehovah's gracious dealings in providence and prophecy were like a continuous training of His son—similar, in fact, to what we ourselves are passing through. If I succeed in this, it ought to become very apparent to you that the Lord has been at your right hand also through your own lives past; that no period in our experience is purposeless or empty of sacredness; but that He Who trains us is striving, with steadfast, tolerant love, to make the most of every one of us, and through the inevitable changes which we undergo from youth to old age, to fit each one of us for the discharge of a noble mission in this world, as well as for the inheritance of a nobler hope in the world to come.

I.

"When Israel was a child," God "called His Son out of Egypt." Perhaps we ought not to say that "the nation was born in a day"—the day of the Exodus. At all events, the education of the infant nation began that day. The age of the Exodus was its childhood, and the desert was its nursery and schoolroom. Then Jehovah "found His people in a desert land, and in the waste howling wilderness; He led him about, He instructed him, He kept him as the apple of His eye."[1] The dealings of the Almighty with Israel when it was a child proceeded on the same lines as your own discipline in early years. For example, He provided for its wants just as your parents did for yours, so that no labour or forethought was called for on its own part. "Heaven lay about it in its infancy." Bread fell into its lap, it knew not whence. Its "water was sure." Its raiment failed not. Love led its steps by day and watched its sleep by night. One might say, its very whims were humoured. Everything came at a wish, as if by magic.

[1] Deut. xxxii. 10.

-Everything was wonderful, and yet the marvels seemed matters of course. Everything spoke of kindness and power, and invited the child to lean on the all-providing Parent.

Then how similar was the instruction of the wilderness to the way in which we teach our children! We stoop to the young mind, and speak in tale or parable, by picture-book and story-book. So God placed His son who came out of Egypt in a school of truth, where sacred lessons were to be gathered from nature, from providence, from example, from emblematic rites and ceremonies, from the gilded furniture and embroidered hangings of His tent, from the Cloud and Voice that bespoke His Presence. Abstract instruction there was none; but He addressed the eye and imagination of a young people through symbolic ritual and a material tabernacle, through form and colour, through flame and thunder-peal. How gracious was such condescension to the ideas of a child! How it seems to bring God home into your own nursery circle, where, after His example, you try to instil into infant minds an awful truth through some simple avenue of tale or picture!

Again: His discipline of law and penalty—was not that, too, exactly such as we were subjected to in our boyhood? The Decalogue is a code for a young nation—short, concrete, peremptory, forbidding such actions as untutored natures are prone to, but hardly penetrating behind overt act into the springs of conduct. The whole legislation bore a similar character, and it was enforced by punishments, sharp, immediate, and conspicuous, such as might carry with them a warning to others. If one broke the sabbath rest, he "died without mercy." When Miriam insulted Moses, she became a leper. Korah was made an example of for rebellion, and Aaron's sons for wilful neglect of a rubric. Because the camp murmured, the plague came. Because the spies disheartened the people, "they died before the Lord." A system of discipline like this, exemplary, educational, visiting with prompt chastisement every act of transgression, but ignoring the nicer shades of guilt, was one which told, in tones a child may understand, that law is law, and that the Lawgiver will not be trifled with. Is not this the ideal discipline for early youth? What other object have the whippings inflicted upon boys? These, too, like the chastisements of Israel in the Book of Numbers, are designed to establish the supremacy of law, to form the habit of submission to authority, and to cure the child of petulance, fickle unreason, and obstinate wilfulness—the faults of young children as of young nations.

II.

Behold, then, after this boyish discipline, the son whom God called as a child out of Egypt has attained adolescence. He stands, stalwart and eager but untried, an unfleshed sword by his side, on the border of the promised land—a picture, to me, of that noble dawn of young manhood, so often to be witnessed when, boyhood scarce over, the youth first awakes to the consciousness of life and its possibilities. The age of Joshua and the conquest was eminently an age of juvenile enthusiasm for a new-found ideal. Flushed with brief ardour, full of unquestioning faith, it thought to conquer its heritage at a rush. Very few years sufficed to overrun the land of Canaan, in a fashion. For wonders had not ceased. To the daring heroes of that host everything seemed easy. Young faith laughed at the impossible. Yes, this is the bright confidence with which a lad first faces the serious tasks of life; and although sober, elderly men smile at its crude ambitions, does not the Book of Joshua teach us how God is in it, how His Spirit inspires and blesses it? It is a stage, though a brief one, in the history of men or nations, and, while it lasts, great things are possible.

Usually it does not last long. The history of Israel reminds us that the time of reaction which succeeds is one of the most perilous in human life. When the enthusiasm which reckoned on an easy conquest has spent itself, yet all is by no means conquered, but " the Canaanite will dwell in the land;" when boyish ardour has to be replaced by manly resolution, and the character has to form itself into settled habits of duty, under the dictation of reason and of conscience, then comes a time of trouble and unsettlement. How often have we seen the fair promise of opening adolescence clouded over! Followed by anarchy in the soul, fitful, with moods of wild lawlessness and moods of wild penitence, the baser and the better natures struggling together in alternate mastery, while the unsubdued passions recognize no king over them, and at times every impulse does what seems good in its own eyes. The long period of the Judges was just such a time of formation. It shows you, on a national scale, what many a young man's career shows likewise—the contest still undecided betwixt loyalty to the will of Him Who revealed Himself in childhood, on the one part, and, on the other, the wayward, passionate instincts of nature. The question is, "Are you, or is Israel, to live a consecrated life of faith in Jehovah and of devotion to His high calling? or will you, shall it, yield to the distracting impulses of the flesh and fall beneath the yoke of alien lords?" It is a stormy time so long as the answer wavers—a time of extremes. Doubt wars on faith, passion with reason, self-will with loyalty. Sometimes revolt against authority is pushed to the length of dissipation and open contempt of God; anon, a spasm of remorse sways the whole soul backward to a Bochim of repentance, amid vows to amend—hearty vows, but soon forgotten. Those who watched Israel through its "iron age" might often have feared that it had flung aside for ever its sacred vocation as the people of Jehovah. And how often do onlookers tremble for the future of young men in a similar crisis! How often do the faithless despair of them altogether!

But if any of you can recognize in the days of the Judges a picture of yourselves, learn this, that God did not forsake His people. You have not kept the lessons of your childhood. You have not been always true to the covenant of your fathers. You have not prosecuted the war which, as a lad, you began against inward evil. Sins which you thought subdued then have since got the better of you. You have stained your soul with excess. You have doubted or denied your Saviour. Still, through it all, the God of your childhood, the Guide of your youth, has been with you—even when, like Gideon, you knew it not. Your intervals of regret were from Him. Your efforts to decide for a holy life He inspired. Partial deliverances from vicious habits He has wonderfully wrought out. And if He seem to keep Himself out of sight as He was not wont to do, it is because He would accustom you now to walk by manhood's faith in the Unseen and manhood's devotion to principle and duty. Happy, thrice happy is the young man who at length does catch anew as in a dream the summons of One Who was not always an unknown God, if only he will respond, "Speak, Lord; Thy servant heareth." Struggling out of this moral anarchy into a settled clarified manhood, sobered into self-respect, let him lay himself, with his matured powers, beneath the sceptre of his own elect crowned King—one Jesus the Son of David.

III.

This brings us to the third period. The monarchy in Israel was its period of adult manhood. Its lessons are for the mature and the middle-aged among us. Can we not learn them too, if we will?

Like the last, this period of life often opens fair; like the last, it is often overcast. Israel, in its adult prime under the first two princes of the house of David, ere yet the nation split, was Israel at its strongest. Then it realized its mission most clearly; it won its widest triumphs; it sung its freshest songs; it came nearest to attaining at least its secular ideal. This typifies the years —ambitious and strong and happy—of a man's early Christian manhood, before too much care has furrowed the brow or sorrow has sprinkled the hair with grey: a time when life, and even Christian life, often appears to be at its fruitfullest and best. The man is mature, and as yet unspoilt. He has still much youthful ardour left; a heart still simple and full of hope, only more resolved, self-restrained, and robust than during the formative years of adolescence. This is a man from whose energy and generous ardour the Church and the world have much to gain. It is in these years that speculation and enterprise are most active. Pregnant schemes are started, and splendid work is done. Say, after the days of doubt and passion are spent, do you know—did you ever know—

what it is frankly and for good to take Christ to be your manhood's King, and fling yourself into His work with a noble ambition to achieve great things, yet withal in a reverent, devout temper? An opulent stage surely in a man's career—beautiful and full of promise!

Did it only last! Sometimes it does. In those few cases—alas, that they should be few!—in which the spirit of the "new monarchy" is faithfully preserved through middle life, and Christ's kingdom continues to be sought with undivided will, there you have a Christian career of exceptional power and usefulness, drawing the eyes of all men. Far more frequently it happens to the Christian as it happened to the people of Israel. Do we not know the misery of a divided rule? It comes to us Christians as it came to Israel. When Israel under Solomon reached its settled maturity as a State, it was brought of necessity into very close contact with the heathen States around. War and trade and politics and art and literature were so many secular elements endangering the simplicity of its early faith and drawing it into the fashions of its neighbours. It was hard then to be in the world, yet not of it. Hard to hold itself in sacred aloofness, as a son of Jehovah brought out of Egypt, with His awful vows upon it, when every day it had to traffic with Egypt and the rest of them; holding relations commercial, diplomatic, social, with the surrounding world that knew not God. To this danger the chosen people succumbed, but in part. Their history from Jeroboam to the Captivity is the history of an intestine strife betwixt the secular and the sacred; betwixt the party that compromised with heathendom and the party that clave to Jehovah. The outward division of the kingdom was both a result and a symbol of this far deeper division in the heart of the nation: deepest division of all, a house divided against itself, a life halting, oscillating, between God and Baal.

Of course, Israel had in consequence a spoilt career. But have not most middle-aged Christians to confess as much? We too, when we settle down in the entanglements of business and domestic life, with politics and society and family cares and a hundred interests of this world soliciting or demanding our attention, find it very hard not to grow worldly. Secret decadence creeps thus on the middle portion of our days. The singleness of youthful ardour for Christ and humanity is exchanged for a dual life, a life of compromise, a life of unworthy concession to the world's way and of feeble protest against it. I am sure we know too well what this means. It is the explanation of many a stunted, colourless, ineffective Christian career. The devout life that gushed like a stream twenty years ago, creeps stagnant in a marsh to-day. The Christian has put on so close a resemblance in every outward respect to the greedy, loveless, godless society around him, that he can scarcely be recognized from it. He conforms to its fashions; he apes its manners; he is infected with its spirit. To discover that he has still a remnant of his old piety left, which keeps up a secret struggle against the deadening worldliness, you need to follow him to his closet, at those times—too rare now—when alone he listens to the voice of God. There, to be sure, prophet-voices are sometimes raised in ineffectual warning. Efforts even at a partial reformation are made from time to time—spasmodic, futile efforts. But the entanglement is too masterful; his life flows on in the channel of the world.

How is it to end? If God the Most Merciful should withdraw His grace from you and say, "Ephraim is joined to idols: let him alone!"[1] then indeed it could end but in one way, and that speedily. But He Who has betrothed us to Himself in faithfulness is of wondrous patience. "How shall I give thee up, Ephraim? How shall I deliver thee, Israel? How shall I make thee as Admah? How shall I set thee as Zeboim? Mine heart is turned within Me; My repentings are kindled together!"[2] With what astonishing perseverance does Jehovah deal with His backsliding people! What a variety of methods does He employ! He it is Who has thus far upheld your better nature, though sadly overborne. He rouses you now and then to consider and repent. There is still a seed of spiritual life in you; for His Spirit has not forsaken you. He "rises early" to send you His messengers, the prophets. By His Word, at His Table, in the prayer-meeting and in the closet, He keeps alive beneath the ashes a yearning after closer fellowship with Christ; nay, even a hope of some better day to come, when you shall be able to shake off the dust of this world and put on the beautiful garments of holy service.

At last it comes to this with many of us (as it came to it with Israel of old) that nothing will do save a chastisement, which by desolating the heart drives you back to God. He "causes all your mirth to cease." He may not literally rob you of your fortune; but, through family losses or ill health, he makes it a portion which can satisfy no longer. Thus He finds a way to break the fatal fascination which this world has been exerting over you. Thus He allures you, metaphorically, into the wilderness, that at the end

---

[1] Hos. iv. 17.   [2] Hos. ii. 20; xi. 8.

He may "speak comfortably" to you, and "take out of your mouth the names of Baalim," and renew His broken covenant of love, and make you to "sing there as in the days of your youth, and as in the day when you came up out of the land of Egypt."[1] Into how many Christian lives that verge towards old age does the divine mercy send a melancholy change, which, like the disaster of the Captivity to Israel, means the disillusioning of worldly dreams and the shipwreck of worldly hopes. Israel learns then that there is no *rôle* for it to play on the stage of this vain world. From the thickening plot of worldly men and the clash of their contending ambitions, God calls His son back to Himself and to the forgotten or abandoned task laid on him in his youth. Then does the valley of trouble become a door of hope. Blessed be His name; for "His mercy endureth for ever!"

IV.

Thus have we reached the last stage whether of a nation or of a man—the stage of decline and decay. The centuries which lay between the Captivity and the fall of Jerusalem constituted the old age of the Hebrew State. They offer at least this parallel to the old age of a Christian, that while void of joy or strength or dignity from a material point of view, they witnessed the unfolding and they closed with the fulfilment of a heavenly hope. Had Israel been a merely secular kingdom, its "decline and fall" would have brought, like that of other States, hopeless ruin. Its career would have ended in a death without any spiritual resurrection or glory to follow. It would simply have been wiped out from the list of Western Asiatic States, absorbed for

[1] Hos. ii. 11-20.

good or ill into some stronger power. But because it was God's son, once brought out of Egypt, and had all along cherished a divine life through its political vicissitudes, therefore it happened to it as to all God's sons: the death of the body was the emancipation of the spirit. The "earthly house of its tabernacle" was taken down only that the hidden life which it contained might be manifested to the world through "a building of God, not made with hands."

Israel in Babylon, abandoning the ambitious projects of a secular State, returned to God. Then it fully conceived for the first time as its national glory the hope of a Divine Messiah, suffering yet triumphant. This hope kept the nation alive; roused it even to fresh exertions; sustained it in martyrdom; flattered it to its latest hour with a passionate longing, full of immortality. Nor did this hope make Israel ashamed. The true Israel, waiting for its consolation, found what it waited for. God's promise was fulfilled. In the midst of temporal decay and collapse there came to the dying nation what in its best moments it had so long desired, what through every change it had been prepared to receive. There came to it its Christ, its Hope, its Consolation, and its Glory. A new and more spiritual life opened before it. Israel after the flesh died; the spiritual Israel of the Church was born.

How similar is the issue of that Christian old age which has learned the lessons of affliction! Taught by painful experience, my aged brethren have ceased to hope much from this world, or to divide their hearts betwixt God and worldly good. In this surrender of earthly ambitions, heavenly hope has been new-born. Aged believers set their affections now on things above. They wait for a promised consolation. They nourish a spiritual joy amid the decay of natural vigour. They long to be with Christ. It may be that this yearning after the sight of their Lord rouses them to labour for His appearing. It may be that it only possesses their soul with a mild and placid patience of hope. Anyhow, it gilds the decline of a Christian's day with a lovely sunset glow, which gives promise of a better morrow. At evening-time it is light. Age has its infirmities; it has its fretfulnesses too; and neither are beautiful to the eye. Nature in a man rebels against the bondage and the humiliation which are the lot of age, just as Israel's pride rebelled against its national degradation when it felt the Roman yoke. Nor do new revelations of truth visit the aged. To them, as to Israel, the voice of the prophet speaks no more. All old men live, like old nations, on their past. But how happy is the aged Christian who, like old Israel, can also live anew in his anticipated future! When death comes to him it means that his Lord has come at last. The moment of the extinction of earthly existence is the very moment for which his whole earthly existence has been one long preparation; the moment for which he has learned to burn with supreme desire. Then Simeon's swan-like song of *Nunc Dimittis* trembles on the dying Christian's tongue; and the close of life, visible, mortal, fleshly, means for him the birth of life invisible, immortal, spiritual. Farewell earth; welcome heaven with Christ!

Brethren, it is a strangely chequered story, wheresoever written—this of the children of God. From birth to death, a thing of changes, with dark threads crossing light ones. Much it has in our own case to sadden and at times to fill us with apprehension, just as when we read it mirrored in our Bibles. But it is a story which keeps its destined end in view from first to last; and that end is salvation. That end it will not miss, for God is in it. How rich in warning is the history I have sketched with rapid hand! Yet how rich, too, in encouragement for young and old and older, is the thought that with His Christian child, as with His child out of Egypt, God abides! He knows the way we have to go. He is faithful to correct, skilful to train, tender to save. He will never leave us till He hath done that good thing which He hath promised—hath formed the Christ within us, the Hope of glory. At whatever stage of the long history we stand—each of us—may God make us faithful! Then shall we pass through all the stages of our life, gathering lessons at every step, until we finish our course with joy amid the mild enduring radiance of our Father's house—the home that needs no sun and knows no night of change.

GUARD THE DEPOSIT.

SERMON VI.

GUARD THE DEPOSIT.

"O Timothy, guard that which is committed unto thee" (R.V.) (or in margin, "Guard the deposit").—1 TIM. vi. 20.

THERE is an old adage which tells us how men walk most safely in a middle path; and I think experience shows that real progress in human affairs lies midway betwixt an unreasoning conservatism on the one hand, which counts everything sacred and final because it is old, and, on the other, a passion for indiscriminate change. Here in England, at all events, we rather pride ourselves upon our wisdom, because it is our method to advance by building upon what we have tried in the past and found sufficient; not flinging away the good which we possess in search of novelty, but holding fast to it, that we may adapt it to fresh requirements, or learn through experience how to use it better.

Whether or not this be the path of wisdom in politics, at least it is so in matters of religious belief and practice. Time was, not a great while ago, when it was desirable to vindicate inquiry into religious opinions which had gained a sanction from tradition. A presumption prevailed in favour of whatever had come down to us as accepted truth —a presumption so strong that it required some courage to justify the least change of usage or of view, nay, even to exercise the Protestant privilege of free inquiry. Not the ancient faith only, but the ancient forms of faith, were counted too sacred to be criticized. Not the virtues merely of our saintly ancestors must be imitated, but their stale usages and their very prejudices. To-day the spirit of change seems to have won a victory so complete, that a heady current has set in towards the opposite extreme. He who promulgates any novel opinion finds more than candid attention; in many minds he finds a predisposition to accept his novelty, as though the presumption were no longer in favour of the old, but in favour of the new. The revolt against tradition and against orthodoxy is a pronounced one, especially with the younger minds. To doubt what has been received, questioning the old because it is old, is a fashion of the hour; not more reasonable than the blind traditionalism to which it has succeeded, and perhaps a good deal less safe; since it affords some men a pretext for sitting loose to all religious belief whatever, and tempts other men to shift their ground on vital questions of faith after next to no serious inquiry, or for the most insufficient and trifling reasons.

Instead, therefore, of needing to-day to justify the right of a Christian to investigate the grounds of his ancestral belief, or to modify in detail the formulas where it is enshrined, what seems to be most called for is a protest against the rash abandonment of ascertained truth, with a firm reminder that everything in Christianity is not open to change—not made to shift and pass away before the advent of modern theories. There is a basis of certain truth and fact—a substantive "faith once delivered to the saints"— which we are not at liberty to barter for novelties. This it is not ours to alter or improve upon, but to "guard;" for it has come down to us as a sacred deposit from the Lord of heaven, and we hold it in trust for those who shall come after us. Nor does the present appear to me an unsuitable occasion[1] for inviting attention to this character of finality, or of permanence, attaching to the central Christian verities. It becomes an old Church, like ours, with a long pedigree and a wealthy heritage of heirlooms in the shape of confessional principles and living traditions, to be cautious how it lets go its hold upon ancient truth, or betrays to a mere craze for unsettlement that which is eternal, that which sustained the spiritual life of past generations, that which we hold in fee for our children, that which is not ours but the Master's—a deposit from Christ committed to our keeping.

When I speak thus, I have in view the substance of Christian and evangelical teaching, which is, thank God! no private possession of ours, but the common treasure of all reformed Christendom—to a large extent of all Christendom; in the maintenance of which every other Church has the same interest as we have. I am not thinking here of forms of worship, or of methods of administering Church business. These, I am quite aware, must admit of useful change as the tastes or habits of men change from age to age. Neither am I thinking of those creeds, more or less venerable, but also more or less antiquated, in which theologians of former days were led to express what seemed to them the truths of Scripture. The Church's manner of conceiving and of expressing truth must necessarily alter to some extent in the course of centuries; and we can easily afford to change the shape of the containing vessel, provided we do not spill the water of life. Nor have I

---

[1] This sermon was preached at the opening of a Church Synod.

even in view those matters of mere opinion which have at one time or other come to be included in the official witness-bearing (say) of an old Church like our own. On not a few subordinate points of belief the views of men may be modified by enlarged study of God's Word or by a wider and truer outlook into the whole horizon of truth, and yet no portion of the Christian faith be really sacrificed. What I am concerned to insist upon may be laid down briefly thus:—

First, that there is a substratum of religious experience and conviction common to Christianity with other religions which cannot change from age to age, because we men of this late century really stand in reference to such elementary spiritual facts of experience precisely where our forerunners have always stood and in no better position.

Next, that because Christianity is an historical and revealed religion there must be a central kernel of Christian fact and teaching handed down to us which is unchangeable, permanent, incapable of being exploded by new discoveries or improved upon by new speculations.

And, lastly, that so far as the substance of what has heretofore been taught as the Catholic faith of Christendom is concerned, while it ought never to decline reinvestigation in a right spirit, yet the presumption in favour of its correctness is enormous; so that it ought not to be lightly abandoned by any serious person.

These points do not need much in the way of explanation.

1. So far as the first point is concerned: the elementary factors of the inner and spiritual life of man with which religion deals are plainly the same from age to age, and

equally accessible at all times. They are matters of constant human experience, lying as near to the earliest as to the latest of mankind. On a thousand subjects, to be sure, we stand on the shoulders of our forefathers; so that, as has been said, a child may know more of the gathered stores of observation and experiment than the wisest of the ancients. It is a fallacy to conclude that it must be the same with moral or religious truth. The inward facts about duty, sin, remorse, repentance, holiness, fellowship with God,—these remain precisely the same for every generation. The personal relations which may subsist betwixt the human spirit and the divine, whether in deprecation of divine displeasure or hope in divine mercy, in obedient reliance on the will of the Unseen or in criminal disregard of it,—these relations are affairs of immediate personal experience, in regard to which all men have to commence very much at the same point. Such things each of us has to learn anew and for himself. God was as close and as real to Abraham four thousand years ago as He is to any man to-day. The oldest of our race might learn within his span of years just as much about the fixed conditions of a soul's inner life as we can do, since these depend upon experience. They become known by living through them; and they come as fresh and entire to each new human being, as do the ever young mysteries of life and death, of joy and pain, of toil and hope, and love and hate. It is on this invariable platform of spiritual facts and truths, written deep within each bosom, that all religions ultimately repose, and Christianity among the rest. So far as this goes, therefore, mankind is likely to make no new discoveries; it gathers little fresh light, but stands to-day where it stood in days gone by.

2. Next, as to the positive light which the Christian Gospel professes to shed upon these underlying questions of personal experience, here is the characteristic feature with which before all we have to reckon: the Gospel is a series of historical facts, or it is nothing. What it declares is, in brief, that the unseen eternal God, at a given date and in a defined way, interposed to solve the permanent problems of the religious life of man. It belongs to Christianity, therefore, that it either stands on certain old unalterable facts, or it does not stand at all. Evaporate the facts and you have nothing left—nothing, that is, which is distinctively Christian, nothing that any other religion will not give you. The attempt which has been often made, and is made to-day, to surrender these facts, and yet retain what is of enduring value in the teaching of Christ and His apostles, is foredoomed to failure; for with the facts the doctrines go, the doctrines being nothing more than an explanation of the facts; and what remains is a residuum of elementary moral ideas about God and human responsibility, common to nearly all religions whatever. I am not to stay here to argue whether the recorded facts of the Gospel narrative, being (as they evidently are) supernatural, can be successfully assailed or not. That is a question I must leave to be discussed at proper place and time. My point is, that until they have been utterly demolished as facts, proved beyond doubt to be historically false, so long must they form a hard unalterable kernel of Christian verity behind which we cannot go; a deposit which we can neither add to nor take from, which is there for us to stand upon, and live by, and guard, just as it was given to the race near nineteen hundred years ago. To these fundamental facts the faith of the Christian Church is pinned fast for ever-

more. It is by no means pinned to a theory about inspiration, verbal or otherwise; or to a certain list of canonical books, all these inspired and not another; or to this book being by such an author and that by such another; or to the absolute reconcileableness of every statement in every Gospel with every other; or to the literal accuracy of all the statements in any Gospel. On points like these men may differ, and though the difference be important in its way, the faith is not shaken. But to the facts that Christ was born of the Virgin Mary, was crucified under Pontius Pilate, rose from the grave, ascended into heaven; to the one central fact covering all the rest—a superhuman intervention of Almighty God to redeem fallen men and restore peace betwixt earth and heaven and give back celestial life to sinners: to this, beyond all doubt, we must stand committed if we are Christians at all.

Every one will admit that such a body of facts presents difficulties in the way of belief, which are greater for the modern mind than they were for our fathers. The literal appearance of a Divine Person upon earth for the purpose of redeeming and rescuing the race from sin and misery, is no doubt a tremendous allegation. Beyond controversy, "great is this mystery of godliness," as it is given us in, perhaps, the oldest written creed of Christians: "He was manifested in the flesh, justified in the spirit, seen of angels, preached among the nations, believed on in the world, received up in glory."[1] Like the (so-called) Apostles' Creed, that New Testament one is, as you see, wholly a string of stupendous facts alleged about one stupendous Person. Nor can we get rid of the admitted difficulty by winnowing some residuum of naked history clear from that

[1] 1 Tim. iii. 16 (R.V.).

theory or doctrine regarding it which lends to the facts their Christian colour. In the Gospel, fact and doctrine are one, tied by a living ligament, so that to cut them asunder is to kill them both. Either Jesus was born of a virgin or He was not; lived a sinless life or did not; rose from the dead or never rose; ascended alive into the sky or did not ascend. If you deny these to be facts, then, to be sure, you have no difficulty left. A Jew named Jesus who was not born of a virgin, was not sinless, however good, and once dead remained dead, need tax nobody's faith very hard. But then you have killed the religion. There is no such thing left you as Christianity; and no accounting any longer for these immense facts of history—Christian life, Christian literature, and the Christian Church. Whereas, if the facts alleged in the Gospel be facts at all, the doctrines of our faith grow out of them by sheer necessity. The Man born of a virgin must be a superhuman Man, a Son of God. The sinless Man, if He died at all, must have given His life for the sin of the world. If He rose and went up, then He must live to save. Facts, do you call such things? But they are more. They are the living seeds of truth with endless power hid in them, and out of them has grown the faith and the theology of Christendom.

Here, therefore, we hit upon a solid core at the heart of the great Christian system, which cannot change with time and the progress of the minds of men or the growth of science. It is a *datum*, or thing given, which has been there from the beginning of the Gospel, and must remain there to the end. What has once happened never varies. The meaning of it you may come to comprehend better as time goes on; but the event itself is past alteration. And if that event be a divine deed, instinct with religious meaning, affecting profoundly the spiritual conditions of life for all men and for all time, then it is clear that your doctrine, as well as your fact, is beyond change, given you for ever. Essentially a final thing, a "deposit" to be kept while the world stands.

3. But now it may be urged: Granting what you contend for, that there is a nucleus of Christian truth circling round the history of Jesus Christ, which is essential and permanent in our holy religion; is it equally certain that theologians have understood it rightly, or that they have not spun from slender materials a vast system of theological speculation with which they have overloaded the creeds of later centuries? To that I reply: He would be a rash man indeed who should deny that matters have been keenly debated in theological controversy and have found their way into some confessions, which are no part of the deposit entrusted to Christendom to guard. But, in the first place, it is not around these matters that interest chiefly turns at the present moment. The present contention of Christians is far more *pro aris et focis*, as the ancients said, for the altar and the hearth—for what is sacred and indispensable in Christian faith. In the second place, the mass of Christian dogma about which no difference arises among the great Christian communions is very much larger than is popularly supposed. Set aside metaphysical difficulties about the origination of the new life in the soul, and one deep feud respecting the powers of the Church, her sacraments, and her ministry, there is scarcely another doctrine of consequence which is not held substantially alike in nearly every Church. That leaves a notable *consensus* in Christendom. Put together these great mysteries: of the Trinity, of the Person of the Lord Jesus, of the fact of His Atonement for

sin, of His elevation to glory with power to save and judge mankind, of the Mission of the Holy Ghost, of the New Birth, of the free Forgiveness of Sins, of the Hope of the Second Advent, of Resurrection, and of Eternal Life for all believers: put these, I say, together, and what a solid body have you of accepted beliefs! These are the most peculiar and influential of all Christian doctrines. About these, Christians are virtually at one. All these they equally prize as the sacred "deposit" entrusted by the Lord to His living Church. With reference to this whole body of beliefs, at all events, the duty of Christians is a clear one. It is not to be held like any slight opinion of the day or merely probable theory, open to be revised or set aside in an hour at the suggestion of some new speculation or liable to be upset by the latest discovery in archæology. Men cannot build their religious confidence on such a shaky foundation as that. Nor is it in the least wise or worthy of serious minds to assume that, while Christianity itself may be true at bottom, all Christendom has gone hopelessly astray in its understanding of its tenets; that the entire body of belief which, from the days of the apostles downward, has inspired the hope and commanded the assent of Christendom, is as likely as not to be, after all, a foolish mistake. On the contrary, there is, as a mere matter of reasoning, an overwhelming probability in favour of what has been believed from the first and by all Christian ages. The chances are that the accepted conclusions of theological science have a great deal to be said for them, and are far too deeply grounded to be overthrown by every wind of modern opinion. To take up ignorantly the "newest thing out" in religion, as one would a fresh discovery, and be ready without inquiry to throw away the most ancient and stable beliefs of Christendom in favour of the latest dream of some brilliant essayist or the hypothesis of a speculator in theology, is really putting a fool's-cap upon reverent and sober inquiry. All Churches owe it to the truth of Christ to protest against such frivolous abandonment of what has come down to us rich with the tears of saints and the blood of martyrs. By all means let the conclusions of the past be open to candid review in the spirit of ripe and accurate scholarship, of sober and cautious science. But do not set light by the most awful verities of our holy religion as if they had only been heard of the day before yesterday, or had not been pondered over by the sages and lived in by the devout of eighteen hundred years. The truths here in question are too sacred, the issues at stake are too fearful, to warrant a flippant rejection of what has hitherto been most surely believed among us. These truths which have come down to us from Christ and His apostles are simply the most precious possessions of the human race. Study them by all means; understand them better; clear them of misapprehension and human error where you can. But beware how you fling away at random, in a hasty hour, any portion of your treasure. It is too costly. It is from God. The life of souls is in it. It carries the hopes of mankind. Let us guard it for His honour Whose truth it is, and Whose great Name is concerned in its pure and wide promulgation. Guard it for your own souls' sake; for it is your life and the one pole-star to guide you out of time's shadows across the broad gulf of death into the Everlasting Land. For your fellows' sake guard it and spread it; for it is the Father's Word to His wandered, sin-sick children—to all the crowds that have lost their way and stumble down, pierced with the thorns of earth, to the darkness of eternity.

LESSONS FROM JACOB'S DREAM.

SERMON VII.

LESSONS FROM JACOB'S DREAM.

"He dreamed, and behold a ladder set upon the earth, and the top of it reached to heaven: and behold the angels of God ascending and descending on it."—GEN. xxviii. 12.

A YOUNGER son driven from his home for his own fault, with no patrimony but his staff and his father's blessing; a solitary march on foot all day by unfamiliar roads across bare and stony hills; nightfall in the vicinity of an alien settlement whose hospitality one is afraid to claim; a hard bed, therefore, on the unsheltered ground, with the jackal's cry making night hideous; for the morrow, fresh danger and anxiety awaiting the homeless wanderer;—it was under circumstances so forlorn as these that heaven opened itself above the dreamer, disclosing a vision of encouragement which not only made despair for ever impossible to Jacob, but has since then shed light at darkest hours into hearts without number.

To-day once more may its ancient lessons drop perchance like a needed balsam on some wayworn and disheartened worshipper. They are such lessons as can hardly come amiss in a world like ours, where crowds of weary feet are treading every day a desolate path that leads them they know not whither.

I.

Never alone and never forgotten before God: here was the first cheerful message of the dream.

The pain of friendlessness, one of the sorest from which the unfortunate suffer, is a pain that at one time or other fastens upon most of us. The country lad when he first sits down alone in his dingy city lodging; emigrants amid the strange foliage of a new world; the shipboy "on the giddy mast," far from that cozy home where his mother's image flits before his fancy, while the waves keep up their idle plash all through his watch by night;—how many more have felt it? Nothing unmans the stout heart or makes the spirit sink like the thought that one is out in the big hard world, alone, without a soul to care whether one live or die.

Similar must be the feeling that comes over a business man when losses threaten his solvency, and he looks round in vain upon his acquaintances for one prepared to stand by him at a pinch with effectual help. Nay, it is possibly this falling off of accustomed props—this being left to one's self and one's own resources—which makes to many a man half the horror of dying.

In all such experience there is no sure relief save in the truth revealed to Jacob, that not one of us at our utmost need is forgotten or forsaken of God. In the deepest night, when stars are quenched, one Eye wakes and sees. In outcast guilt, when not a creature will take your part or speak a word for you, one Heart above is pitiful. In extremity when it seems as if no earthly power could save, one mighty Friend, Helper of the helpless, is at hand to bend over the abandoned and despairing. Often it is in the most unlikely places that this delicious thought of the near presence of God comes like a revelation to the soul. The youth sits week after week in his father's pew for years, and takes all the blessed teaching of religion as a thing of course. Not till he must go out with his staff and bundle to be a wanderer in the world, does the God of his fathers become to him a surprising and awful Reality. Then the lonely spot grows on a sudden instinct for him with a Presence of which till then he has only heard men tell; and in the awakening of his soul to this new discovery, he can but cry out, "How dreadful is this place! God was in this place, and I knew it not!"

All places are dreadful enough had we but eyes and ears for the Most High. But it is a dreadfulness this which shuts out meaner alarms and occupies the soul with a great calm. Dear soul, get to be right familiar with the Divine Presence. It is a friendly shade. It is a stronghold for defence. It is a refuge for the hunted, a pavilion for the weary, and a home for the exile. "He that dwelleth in the secret place of the Most High shall abide under the shadow of the Almighty. . . . He shall cover thee with His feathers, and under His wings shalt thou trust."

II.

Betwixt earth and heaven there lies an open pathway, is the second consoling message, taught by the dream of that "Syrian ready to perish."

The second is required to supplement the first. That God sees us in our solitude, cares for our distress, and bends over us in our need, is something, is much; for it means that we are neither friendless nor forgotten. But it is far more to be told that, although betwixt His pity and our extremity there yawns the whole distance between heaven and earth, yet that is not, as we might fear, an unbridged chasm. It is a gulf which love can span, which succour can traverse. Heaven is far off, but its windows will open. Heaven is far off, but on earth there is a gate that leads to it. A road lies thither along which messengers of help can pass and repass. A road even by which mortals may climb; for see, there is a stair, and the foot of it is here beside us, while the top of it reacheth unto heaven.

In naked words, there is no man so far from aid that God cannot find ways to rescue or befriend him. To preach this cheering truth with authority and make it live in our hearts by example after example, is that which makes the Bible of all books the book for the unhappy. Hagar in the wilderness of Et-tih was alone; but God saw. Joseph in the pit was resourceless; but God preserved him. Jonah at the bottom of the Mediterranean seemed cut off from intercourse; yet God heard. Daniel in the lions' den was without defence; God became his Deliverer. Peter in Herod's dungeon looked only for death; God sent His angel and saved him. Such instances abound. It is our extremity which creates an opportunity for the Almighty; and as you must extinguish your lamp if you would see the stars, so it is in the thick darkness of a trouble which no earthly ray relieves that heaven will open above a man's head its wonderful window, and let down to his feet its ladder of escape.

For all of us it is of essential consequence that we learn to walk through life by the faith of this royal truth. By the faith of it, I say; for it is not a truth which we can expect to see by the light of "common day." When the East grew red with dawn, arousing that sleeper, the opened sky and the shining staircase and the happy angels all fled away. Clear day showed him nothing more than a chalky road and a stony hillside. But do you think the desolate landscape could look equally uninhabited or cheerless after the vision as before? Was the sky over Jacob's head as brazen and fast closed when he pressed forward on his way? or God as far off? or the mountain-path as unfrequented? Did no presences haunt next day's journey save the whirr of the startled quail or the spring of the jerboa? I think other wings than those of the wild bird beat the air around him. Unseen forms hovered near. As often as he glanced upward to the burning azure, was there not within its depths a glory more splendid than the sunlight? Depend upon it, when heaven has once opened itself to a man, it can never be quite shut again. The ladder does not really depart when the vision ceases. God is still felt to be over us though we see Him no more; and messengers of His grace keep coming still and going, through the "garish day" and the starless night alike. We shall not behold them with our eyes. In the faith of them we have to walk, counting on their assistance, "until these shadows flee away."

Under what guise the visitants from heaven became recognizable to the patriarch in his nocturnal vision, I do not know. Of one thing we may be sure, God need never be at a loss for messengers. That the unmetaphorical prose of the New Testament is to be read quite literally when it tells of "ministering spirits sent forth to minister to the heirs of salvation," just as they ministered to the Captain of salvation Himself, I see no reason to doubt. The happy childlike faith of the ancient Church in strong, pure guardians out of the Invisible, bending in tenderness over the cradle of slumbering childhood or sustaining with unseen arm the steps of manhood in noble enterprises, seems to me a belief which conflicts with no ascertained fact. It embodies a thought too precious as well as beautiful to be lightly surrendered. But—angels or no angels—our Lord has servants enough to do His errands. He makes the winds to be His messengers, and the flaming fire His minister. All things in earth or heaven stand at His service Who is Head over all things for His Church's sake. All of them will wait upon the man "whose heart is pure, whose hands are clean;" according to that sweeping generalization of St. Paul, "All things are yours; for ye are Christ's, and Christ is God's."

In disguise such angels come. Every true man finds that his blessings reveal themselves out of a dark cloak. Through unwelcome hands, of poverty, sickness, loss, or mental gloom, God sends us our choicest benefits. Nor is the soul's intercourse with the Unseen often so lively or so fruitful as when in life's pilgrimage we light, like another Dreamer, upon "a certain place where was a den." Once for all, then, let us learn to keep our spirits open to the angels. Things are not what by the daylight of this world they seem to be. God reserves a road of His own—secret, but patent—to the soul of every man. By any agency, through any channel, He can send the succour He designs for His child. Only let the heart be possessed with a settled persuasion that His ladder still stretches up to an open heaven, as it used to do, and we may go our way alert and expectant of unseen blessings. It is good to bid the din of this world be still and hush the voices of the soul herself, that in solitude and silence we may cultivate that intercourse with the Eternal which is the hidden strength of all moral life. Nor let us be chary to entertain what guests soever God may send, even though they offer a "vinegar aspect" or wear a sable garb. In bidding sorrow welcome, or pain, or opprobrium, has not many a man "entertained angels unawares"?

III.

Faithful to His covenant-promise is our fathers' God: this is a third lesson fairly to be gathered from the midnight epiphany vouchsafed to Jacob.

It was not by haphazard that over this man's pillow of all men, or on that night of all others, did Heaven disclose its favours. This guarantee of divine protection, assuring the wayfarer that his father's God would be his God, stood in the line of earlier revelation, and in its turn prepared for later. Of the amazing contract of Deity with his grandfather, Jacob was heir at the second remove. The birthright and blessing of this sacred inheritance he had just secured at his brother's expense; but he had secured it by dishonourable means. One can hardly suppose the man's conscience failed to smite him that heavy day, when, thrust forth by a mother's hand, he fled from a brother's revenge. Would it be surprising if, when he laid his head upon the stone, his soul was darker than the sky by night? Must it not have been with him a grave question how far he dared to reckon on the mercy of his father's God after the sin that he had sinned, or presume on the fulfilment of promises of which he had proved himself unworthy? To misgivings of this sort the midnight dream carried a reply. It said that God will not disown His plighted word even to the undeserving, but can still be a God to men whose past is unworthy of His grace. This meant no condoning of duplicity and selfishness. The supplanter of his brother had a long and bitter course of discipline to live through before he fully learnt the baseness of his conduct, or wrestled out a victory over himself, or purged the stain of guilefulness from his nature. So have we all a lifelong education before us ere we can be counted worthy of the friendship of God.. But the encouragement of that night's discovery lies here—that God is content to receive us into His covenant just as we are, if only we are content to enter the school of His discipline. As we are, He will own us and take us in hand. No blot of the past will be a disqualification—no, nor any inbred twist of disposition. For by the patient ministry of His providence, and the ascending and descending messengers of His grace, He is prepared to train and purify and ennoble the worst of us, aiding us in our sore contest against evil nature, until He can crown us at the last as princes with God who have overcome.

Would that my voice could reach the leaden ear of any who, having fallen from innocence, are afraid to claim the promises of the gospel! You too may be the son of a pious father; you may cherish the memory of ancestors who in their day walked with God. So far as lineage can establish any claim on Heaven, you stand in the natural line of its blessings. But since you grew to responsible age, how have you violated the covenant of your infancy! Early habits have been cast off, or religious profession has been treated as a mask, till now you feel as though the sweet words of the gospel were no longer for you, a wanderer, almost an outcast, from the dwellings of the people of God. Ah, let the old dream bring home its message—that God did not forget you when you turned your back on Him; that grace is for the graceless; that He is a Friend to the undeserving still, and will send ministers of help and comfort to the saddest or the loneliest of His prodigal children! Welcome such hopes of mercy. Let holy thoughts, penitent and trustful and tender thoughts from out a better bygone life, revisit your sad heart. They come like white-winged angels, from on high. Vow afresh your vows to your fathers' God. Take Him with you on the way you go. Suffer Him to be your Guide. He will restore you, and educate you into virtue, and change the very heart within you, your Jacob-heart, into the heart of "an Israelite indeed," a saint "without guile."

IV.

This suggests the last lesson I shall connect with Jacob's dream: *The dream has been fulfilled.*

It was a far-off descendant of the patriarch who once under a fig tree in Bethsaida was pondering (as I suppose) the unexplained secret—How can the Holy One stoop in His grace to the unholy? That divine ministries do attend the steps of men as weak and mean and false as any of us had been good news to many since it came to Jacob. But it had always been strange news none the less. For it was hard to reconcile that message of divine favour with the oracle to the truth of which every conscience gives response: "God is of purer eyes than to behold evil." On that spring day a new light dawned upon the ancient problem. In the "good thing" which then came to him out of Nazareth, Nathanael was compelled to recognize no mere plant of earthly virtue, shooting up towards heaven, but a heaven-descended Helper let down in mercy from the Most High. Here was a living Ladder to link the sundered sinner with his God; stairway of descent and ascent, with its foot standing even where we stand, while yet its top reacheth unto the very seat and throne of the Eternal. By Him unto this hour the angels come and go; as by a broad and open bridge spanning the gulf, traversed incessantly by ministers of grace. Which of Heaven's benefits is too precious to descend on our Divine Head? Which of us sinners is too evil to ascend by Jesus' merits to the Father above?

Thus the vision of Bethel has been translated into more glorious fact. Its lessons shine for us with a holier light. So long as the Incarnate Son, our Mediator with God, dwelt on earth, think how angels of power and healing passed down by His sacred Person to the waiting crowds: passed to the maniac, to the palsied, to the dead. So soon as He went back to God, leaving open His track behind Him, think how better angels still, the messengers that fetch to the souls of men Heaven's choicest gifts, descended on the little Church of the Crucified, bearing in their hands repentance, and absolution, and peace, and holy courage, and divinest patience, and charity that thinketh no evil. And still they come. To your own hearts, brethren, they will come this day, if to the Father of mercy you lift up through the Son of man your earnest longing cry. Let not this sacred and fruitful exchange betwixt earth and heaven languish! Leave not God's living Ladder an unfrequented pathway. "By Him we have access in one Spirit unto the Father." See that through His priestly hands your petitions go up without ceasing, your sighs and songs, like the odours of a censer borne by angel-hands into the courts of heaven, into the presence of the King! Then shall the angels return upon you while you pray, laden with benedictions.

OUTSIDE A CLOSED DOOR.

SERMON VIII.

OUTSIDE A CLOSED DOOR.

"Behold, I stand at the door, and knock: if any man hear My voice, and open the door, I will come in to him, and will sup with him, and he with Me."—REV. iii. 20.

It is in the sense of an invitation to deepened intercourse with Christ that I venture to take these words from the Laodicean Epistle.

I do not forget what precious use the Church has long made of them to win the unbelieving. I know how true it is that at hearts the doors of which never opened to Him at all, but are close bolted ever since birth, and overgrown now with a wild tangle of passion and vice, the Saviour patiently stands—His voice heard, though His face is never seen. For all that, it was not to the world, but to the Church, that these words were first addressed. The call to renewed and closer fellowship sent to lukewarm Christians at Laodicea may very well be listened to by every Christian soul. With none of us is the communion which we maintain with our Lord so constant or so intimate as He would have it to be. In such communion it has pleased Him to place our supreme blessedness. Nor ought this to surprise any, since He condescends to regard it as essential, not to our happiness only—which it well might be—but even to His own. The deepest Scriptures indicate as features in our Saviour's character this mysterious craving for the fullest union with His people and the mysterious joy which it imparts to Him. As if love, even in the self-sufficient state of this Lover, could not rest till it had clasped hands with answering love.

I.

Let us first attend to the circumstances under which this invitation may be appropriately addressed to a Christian.

It is plain from the attitude of our Lord outside a shut door, and from His call to open it, that there has been a limit put to the soul's intercourse with her Saviour, and a barrier opposed to His fuller entrance. The Lord Jesus, it seems, is not yet everywhere present in the man. He is not made welcome to the disciple's entire confidence, nor is the life laid open without reserve to His influence. At some point there is withholding or resistance.

Does not this describe fairly enough any stage of Christian experience between our first coming under the power of Christ and our perfection in Christian holiness? Of whom of us is it not true that there remains some region of character or of activity which we have not yet suffered divine grace to occupy? Let the hallowing virtue of Christ have penetrated ever so far, it is not quite coextensive with experience. A certain domain lies still unchristianized—habits, features of character, peculiarities of temper, or favourite pursuits.

The nature of man, indeed, is figured in the text as a house of many chambers, at every door of which the Lord of the mansion must knock for admission. No doubt there is a sense in which you can say that if He is admitted at all, it must be to the innermost of the heart, with acknowledged right to enter and to rule in every part. Yet a man may own such a right of access or of mastery on Christ's part without at once yielding to Christ's exercise of it. Some take to do with the Saviour in a merely ceremonious, or as it were business, fashion. Driven by stress of weather to undo the fastenings of the great outer gate, where too long one kept Him standing, one may transact for one's hereafter with just that distant degree of trust which suffices to sustain a hope of salvation. I think I hear Christians talk of their Lord as of a comparative stranger, Whose help, to be sure, they cannot do without, but Whom they only fall back upon when sore pressed or in straits of conscience. What doors remain still closed against Him! The workroom where we store up life's cares, and may often be found, bent with toil, hugging images of gold. Within that, are statelier apartments set apart for social hours. Still more within, do I not see you withdraw at leisure to a cheery chamber of domestic intercourse where your household gods dwell? It is bright with fireside light, and no unwelcome foot profanes it. But He is not there. Most unbecomingly is He left to ask admission where He ought to be the familiar Inmate, Whose law regulates, while His presence chastens into purity, your family ties.

Innermost of all, and closed by muffled doors, stands the real *sanctum*—the closet of unshared thoughts, secret imaginings, and personal ambitions. Here sits the soul, silent and alone, pursuing unchecked its proper bent and play. Yet even at this sacred door, where no earthly intimate may enter, does Jesus knock. Perchance you keep that dark room for shameful images, or for the weaving of forbidden dreams, or for the worship of a vanished treasure. Can it be that it is like the chamber with its door built up which Ezekiel saw, on whose blind walls were portrayed "every form of creeping and evil things," and within whose guarded secrecy the ancients of the house of Israel sent up incense, "every man in the chambers of his imagery"?

I might name other apartments; but I care not how you choose to label those divisions of our complex life out of which our Lord is excluded. Count over the occupations that fill up each working day, and say how far you let Christ legislate for them all. Glance round the circles of society with which business or amusement brings you into contact, and ask yourself how far your intercourse with each is regulated by the will of your Lord. You may find on inquiry that you are keeping religion too exclusively to the intellectual or to the devotional side of your nature, not suffering it to express itself sufficiently in active duty. Or you may find it to be an affair of fuss and display with you, penetrating hardly at all to the base of character so as to sweeten your temper or restrain your appetites. It may be some favourite study or pastime, from your indulgence in which you have hitherto shut out the thought of God. Or you may not be consciously withholding any department of your life from divine control, and yet you may stand all the while on a cold or distant footing with One Who seeks personal intimacy and a place not second to the closest and dearest of earthly lovers. Of this be sure, that at every shut door Jesus knocks. He will have the freedom of the whole house; will hold all its keys; will enter where we enter, sit where we sit, listen to us, speak with us, be our Comrade and our Confidant in everything. It is His ambition to fill the many-chambered life of man in all its corners with an odour of sanctity and train every one of its activities into the order of heaven.

II.

This leads me to speak next of the demand which, under such circumstances of partial exclusion, our Lord makes upon us.

It is plain that, as I have said, Christ is not content to be on such terms with any of His. Not for His own sake merely. Although it must be for Him a sad thing— a thing which cuts Him to the heart—that we should trust Him so little as not to care to take Him along with us in everything we do, yet it is, I should think, less for His own sake than for ours that He is vexed. Ours is the loss. He comes with blessings in both hands. This Prince of Love has help and healing for every part of us. He longs for leave to crown the work He has begun; to cleanse, and subdue, and elevate, and sweeten, and make glad the whole of our life. It is our unwillingness to open up to Him, and nothing else, which checks the current of His benefactions, and reduces Him to stand, with hands still "laden" and half His kindly purpose unfulfilled, a suppliant Saviour.

Yet He will do no more than knock and call. Though the urgency is on His side, He will not open. Though as crowned King He stands, with title to command and power to compel, yet He will not open. Though the evil done within doors may be as gross as His pity is surely great, He will not open. To the latest step in spiritual life, as at its earliest, God will do no violence to man's reluctance; nor does it beseem One Who draws near in grace, ungraciously to force a passage. Nor, in truth, can the door to our heart's affections be broken through from without, only opened consentingly from within. Permission He must crave; He cannot and He will not enter undesired.

One day, I know, He will in a more masterful fashion break a way through every bolted gate, to startle with His presence the conscience of the impenitent; to flood each dark chamber of memory with the light that rebukes; to trample down the idols and drag abominations out to view. But it will be in the day of His indignation, when He needs no longer to stand on ceremony or petition as a Suppliant the obdurate will of His creature. Then, without leave asked, shalt thou lie bare, exposed to the Searcher of all hearts, and tremble at the entrance of His no longer lingering feet.

But now it is affectionate welcome He craves. He waits upon the turning of thy will, the unbolting of thy door. Why need we wonder at the raggedness of any Christian's character, or the fitful tediousness of his sanctification? No doubt there do come hours when at the breath of God heart-doors unfold, as at the soft south wind of summer the rose-leaves open. Then Christ's warmth pours in to the centre of one's being, and all its graces ripen. But this must be when He makes us willing in a day of His power. Who that knows the reluctance of his own will can wonder why the character of good men displays so many lifelong inconsistencies; why the growth of the inward life is broken by dreary interruptions when piety stands still; or why large tracts of conduct lie for years unreclaimed for God, or unreformed by the Spirit of Christ? Who can wonder at anything but that the Sanctifier does not weary at His thankless task?

Perhaps the limits we all set to the presence of Christ

in our life will cease to surprise us, if we reflect what it means to admit Him there without reserve. It implies that we consent to be criticized and to be interfered with in everything. Not only does He come with eyes of flame, to scrutinize our motives and judge even our secret wishes by a standard of absolute right. To be laid bare in His light is trying enough for every one, save the most humble and most sincere lover of goodness. But that is not all. He will not play the *rôle* of an idle onlooker. Open to Him, and His hand reaches down through your very being with energy in it both to destroy and to reconstruct. The Divine Presence is exacting; it can neither recognize imperfection nor tolerate resistance. When you invite, therefore, a Divine Guest, you must reckon with the consequences. He comes to command. He comes to smite down whatever He dislikes. He comes to make His own will done in everything. He comes not alone, but with His court about Him—stern-faced duties and meek-eyed graces in His train, for all of which room must be found. Nor does He come for brief stay, but to set up His realm within you, and dwell there and rule for ever.

Is it strange that men hesitate, even Christian men, to open up their whole inner nature, with all the cherished habits of their life, to the inspection and interference of One so lordly in His demands? Before we do so, it must have come to this—that we cannot do without Him. Again and again in the course of Christian experience, as at its origin, a conjuncture arrives when the soul is in despair for want of what her Lord alone can do for her. Something is wrong, so seriously wrong as to baffle and humble the soul and drive her to her wits' end; then only is she fain to hear His knock, to undo the bars which pride and custom have made fast, and, falling prone before Him, to beseech Him with tears to take His rightful place within, to search the life that He may change it, to change it that He may abide its Lord henceforth.

It would be wise for all of us to open thus. To give Him now the greeting Eleazar got from Laban: "Come in, Thou Blessed of the Lord; wherefore standest Thou without?" To have Him in to cleanse the temple of our heart with the old Jerusalem cry: "Blessed is He That cometh in the name of the Lord!"

> "Lord, come away;
> Why dost Thou stay?
> Thy road is ready; and Thy paths, made straight,
> With longing expectation wait
> The consecration of Thy beauteous feet!"

III.

A few words may be added in conclusion on the results which ensue from the soul's admission of Jesus Christ to fuller possession of His rights.

So soon as any one is moved to invite a closer intercourse with the Lord in regard to any department of life, instantly its bearings are changed. An altered light falls on the familiar situation, which makes it altogether new. I see now how it affects my Lord, and how He enters into it along with me; and my own attitude toward my environment is modified in consequence. The bad stands rebuked; the good is transfigured. Duty looks easier, and evil hatefuller, when He is by. As though He should enter this room in bodily presence to kindle every face with a radiance from His own and diffuse an awful sacred gladness at being so near a Friend so heavenly, just so does His realized presence in contact with everyday affairs. Its effect is sudden, almost magical. It turns common things to beauty. It reveals a dignity in life we were not aware of. It lifts the soul above meanness and the spell of passion and unworthy fear to a serener and more courageous elevation. It turns doubt into confidence, as it did to Thomas; weeping into rapture, as to Mary; sad hearts to burning, as to the two disciples; and barren toil by night into wealthy blessing at the dawn, as to the Seven by the sea.

For He never comes empty-handed. Without, He stands suppliant and alone. Admit Him: He is the King attended, dispensing royally splendid gifts. He enters to share His own with us. He Who begged leave to be our Guest, saying, "Open unto Me," becomes Himself the Entertainer. 'Tis He Who spreads the table, as the weary fishers learned when, on the beach, ere ever they could fetch of the fish which they had caught, they found a fisherman's meal prepared by the strange Visitor. Nor is He the Purveyor only: He is the Provision of the Supper. For He is so richly provided that He only needs by His Spirit's secret ministry to share with each of us something of His own, and the want of each is fully met. If you can calculate what that means—how one needs to be chastened, another cheered; how He must melt the hard and mould the melted; how some lack probity, and others constancy, and others guidance; how here a martyr is to be kept heroic in the fire, and there a sick child soothed to patience in its crib; how sagacity must inspire the counsels of His Church, and ardour glow in her pulpits; how, in a word, the endless shifting necessities of every Christian and of the whole body are to be suited, century after century:—then you will learn something of the boundless capabilities of the Church's Head.

Nor is all the giving on one side. He takes as well as gives. With One so condescending and communicative, the blessed soul in whom Jesus dwells ventures to be open too. With happy boldness you begin to tell Him everything. You consult Him even in trifles. You lay great and little cares on Him. You ask His aid in every affair. And whatever He enables you to do becomes an offering which goes back to Him again in grateful love. Thus He shares in all of yours as you in His; and communion attains completion. When such an exchange of sweet and secret actings on one another becomes the habit of the inner life, then these two grow together—the soul and her Saviour—inweaved into each other, till neither can be at any moment satisfied without the other's presence, nor is to be thought of as sundered or alone. When such interpenetration of the divine and human partners shall have reached perfection, it will be earth no longer, but heaven. Already He desires it, if we do not. Even in the partial form of it which is possible below, it admits of indefinite degrees of intimacy. Under any form or degree it brings to him who has it the very blessedness of life. Is not this to "sit down in the kingdom of God"? This action and reaction, this varied play of friendship, this sense of common possession, this familiar commerce of giving and receiving, —what else is this but the joy of "supping with Him and He with us"?

Come in, Thou Saviour-King, Who art knocking at our very souls this day for leave to show us all Thy love, come in and traverse these unclean chambers of our being! Purge them by Thy blood. Enlighten their darkness. Fill their empty spaces with Thy riches. Make what is ours, Thine. See, we give it unto Thee—infirmity, error, sorrow: bear it with us! Make what is Thine, ours. See, we open ourselves wide for it—pardon, strength, gladness: share Thy blessings with us! So shall we sup with Thee and Thou with us; till in this communion our spirits echo after their poor measure that ever-sounding song which circles round Thy heavenly banquet-hall—

"Worthy is the Lamb That was slain to receive power, and riches, and wisdom, and strength, and honour, and glory, and blessing!"

JESUS AND BARABBAS.

SERMON IX.

JESUS AND BARABBAS.

"Not this Man, but Barabbas."—St. John xviii. 40.
"We have no king but Cæsar."—St. John xix. 15.

THE cause of Jesus is the cause of a kingdom of God on the earth. With His claims upon men is bound up the real hope of mankind, the hope of ever seeing reared up a universal realm of justice, peace, and brotherly kindness. It is for this that the best of men in every age have laboured. It is the one thing which to the most earnest-minded of our race has made tolerable the frightful evils of existing society—has made life itself worth living. In our own century more than in any previous one this ideal of Jesus Christ has become the accepted ideal of thoughtful men everywhere. It is our one antidote to pessimism. If the world were never to be better than it is, nor an end put to its strifes, wrongs, vices, and cruel passions, what would remain to a noble or sensitive mind except despair? But throw away Jesus Christ and His claim to rule, you throw away your sole chance of such a kingdom of God on earth. He not only represents the true idea of such a kingdom; He alone has the true method of realizing it. If we will let Him redeem society in His own way, He will conduct us, through the quiet endurance of love and the power of an inward Spirit of holiness, to a complete victory of good over evil. But refuse Him, as His countrymen did, and you have but two alternatives before you: either to renounce the hope of an ideal future altogether, or to pursue it by false methods; either to acquiesce in the present supremacy of selfish power, or to revolt against it with selfish violence; either to submit to unprincipled authority, or wade through blood to an anarchy that would be worse; either to have no king but Cæsar, or to choose Barabbas for your saviour.

On the day of our Lord's great rejection by His countrymen, both of these fatal alternatives were chosen; the one by the mob, the other by the prelates.

I shall begin with the latter, the sceptical aristocrats who coolly flung away all hope of a kingdom of God, when they answered Pilate, "We have no king but Cæsar!"

No doubt it is impossible to believe that these chief priests, Sadducean heads of the official hierarchy as they were, meant honestly what they said. They said it to gain their end of terrifying the Roman governor into compliance through fear of delation to the emperor. That they could say it at all shows how hard driven they were. For what did their words amount to? Why, to the renunciation of Israel's Messianic hope! That is to say, they deliberately and in set terms flung away what had been the glory of their race, the immemorial expectation of their countrymen; that which alone gave meaning to their splendid national history, alone inspired its patriot struggles for independence, alone made Israel God's chosen people, an object of His age-long care and the bearer of His blessings to mankind. It is scarcely possible to conceive how any Jew could be so dead to Jewish feeling as, for any end whatever, abjure Israel's Messiah to fawn like a slave at the feet of Tiberius. I do not forget that the words may possibly have been spoken to Pilate alone, in Pilate's antechamber, and not within hearing of the mob, who might for such words have been ready to tear their rulers to pieces. Nor do I forget that these men were playing their last move to checkmate the governor, or that, in threatening him with Cæsar's vengeance if he "let this Man go," they were obliged to pose as themselves friends to Cæsar. Still, it was a novel attitude for Jewish rulers, and Pilate takes his revenge on them by making the most of it. If he is to execute an innocent man in order to prove his own loyalty to his master at Capri, they who force him to it shall make profession of their loyalty no less loud. It is the wily Roman who snaps this trap down on them, and compels them to surrender everything their nation prized as the price of Jesus' blood. No; if they will not have this Man to reign over them, neither shall they have any other, save the emperor. If not this harmless enthusiast for a Messiah, then none at all. The words must out, "We have no king but Cæsar!"

Making due allowance for all this, I do not believe that these priests could have said the words, had faith in the promised kingdom of Messiah, that is, in a kingdom of God, been really alive within them. No Pharisee could ever have used such language. The true Israel who waited for the consolation would not. Even the mob that was shouting for Barabbas outside would not. These priests were sceptics at their heart; Sadducees who believed neither in spirits nor in the resurrection; materialists therefore and secularists, to whom the religious hope of a hereafter meant little or nothing. And because they had lost faith in a living presence of God with men, as well as in the rewards or penalties of the eternal world, therefore they cared for nothing so much as for the maintenance of their own political power. For present security they were ready to renounce the hope on which earnest natures feed—the prospect and the promise of a reign of God among men.

It is an evil omen for an age of materialism. When the heart of any generation is honeycombed with scepticism, and cannot be convinced either that the Eternal lives in active contact with human spirits now, guiding the affairs of this world for His own ends, or that in the awful hereafter men are to reap the fruits of their probation here, how will you keep that generation faithful to any noble ideal of a divine kingdom upon earth? Especially, how will you get those who have anything to lose, to make sacrifices for such an ideal? Christ from heaven to be our Divine King? It is a dream. A kingdom of God that shall be stronger in its feebleness than the Roman empire,—how can a Sadducee believe in that? Let go our place and power here, secured to us by Roman law, and risk the loss of income and of a lordly mansion on Mount Zion should this revolutionary Jesus have His way,—why should a Sadducean aristocrat hazard all that? Against the hard facts and necessities of one's political position, the pious dream of a kingdom of God must shatter! It is not well, perhaps, to speak of it openly, for the words might shock the public ear, even if they do not blister one's own lip; but it is in the heart for all that. We *can* have no heavenly King; no other king, when it comes to the pinch, but this earthly Cæsar.

With the comfortable or ruling classes in any society you will find it come to this, that when religious belief is abandoned, a divine ideal for society goes with it, and the object for which everything is sacrificed comes to be, to keep things as they are—to keep them, that is, in the condition which best suits one's self. In all change there is danger. Why should we court that danger, unless we believe there is a diviner order and a better condition possible for human beings—a redemption or a regeneration or a reconstruction on which God Almighty has set His heart, and which He has sent His Christ to effect? No doubt, if we do believe that, it will be hard to sit still and do nothing, and let (not well, but) *ill* alone—very hard. Towards a real kingdom of heaven, if they believe it is coming, men will press at heavy cost and risk, upsetting many things and spilling many fortunes in the operation. But towards what?—a phantom millennium, in which one can't believe; who that has anything to lose will risk it for that?

Such contentment as this with the existing order of things, such supreme deference to those secular forces which appear to be the strongest thing in our world, you see in whole classes of society; you may see it in yourself. If you yourself believed in Jesus Christ, and that He was alive and present with you, and that He meant to set up a veritable rule of God over you and your neighbours—a state of perfect righteousness, peace, and joy; would it not stir you up to some discontent with things as they are, and some eagerness to mend them, and some effort to change your own life and that of others? Would the placid rule of King Cæsar, of this all-powerful empire of custom and fashion and money—in short, of the world that now is—appear quite so satisfying? Even you might begin to cry after a change, a moral revolution, and to say, We will have another king than Cæsar—" one Jesus!"

The choice of the multitude was a less ignoble one than that of the priests. The leaven of Sadducean unbelief had not spread among the common people. They, therefore, had no mind to bow the knee contentedly to the Roman emperor, however irresistible he might seem to be. Loyal as ever to its hope of divine help, the populace clung to its idea of a Messiah—its false idea—even while it was passionately refusing the true one. Inside the palace, prelates and counsellors, to secure their own place and power, were bartering away the glory of Israel. Outside, there rose louder the hoarse voice of the people themselves—that voice which was then to turn the scale, and has since then grown to be of so much more account in the world's affairs. The mob of the capital made its own choice: "Not this Man, but Barabbas."

We shall miss the point of their selection and lose its lesson if we set Barabbas down for a criminal of an ordinary type. He was a political prisoner. The measures which the Roman government had adopted in Palestine ever since it assumed sovereignty, and especially since Pilate became governor, had wounded the religious and patriotic susceptibilities of Israel to such an extent that the whole land was in agitation. Disaffection was universal, and numerous popular risings took place. It was in one of these *émeutes* that this Jew had distinguished himself as a leader and won popular favour. Such men were fanatical and dangerous. Proscribed by the authorities, they took to an outlaw or brigand career in self-defence. Reckless of their own life, they did not scruple at taking life. But it is a grave error to confound men of this description, who commit crime for an idea, believing themselves to be the leaders of a forlorn hope or martyrs in a sacred cause, with the ruffian who robs or murders for private ends. Such was the class to which I take Barabbas to have belonged; and from this point of view the enthusiasm of the mob for his liberation is at once intelligible and significant. With this class of men our own recent experience both on the continent of Europe and nearer home has unhappily made us too familiar. We know what it means, when they excite public sympathy, when their deeds are whitewashed, if not applauded, and their escape from the clutches of the law is hailed by the populace as a triumph. Did not Pilate comprehend what these shouts meant that demanded the life of the insurgent leader? Does not every government know well what it means when violence directed against established order comes to be screened by a disaffected people? It means that a wild longing for change has begun to burn in men's minds, and that a false hope is luring them on to seek through crime for some better social condition, some imaginary ideal that shall remedy once for all the evils of the present.

"History repeats itself;" and the blunder which that crowd made in Jerusalem when it refused the true Deliverer to choose a false one, is a blunder that is being committed to-day by many ardent hearts in Europe. The choice which was laid that Friday before Israel, practically lies to-day before our modern world. If ever any age (since the Hebrews lost heart) has believed in a better social condition that is bound to come, or has been impatient to attain it, it is the age we live in. But what grieves so many Christians to the quick is just this, that in the nineteenth century, as in the first, men's ideal is still so far from the divine one, and their methods for reaching it so unlike those of Jesus Christ. It may be some contribution towards a just way of looking at many modern questions if we ask ourselves wherein precisely lay the contrast between Barabbas and Jesus, between the ends they severally aimed at and the plans they pursued to reach them. How did the Messiah whom Israel believed in and saved from the stake, differ from the Messiah Whom Israel rejected and sent to crucifixion?

To work out an answer to this would certainly consume more time than you can spare me near the end of a sermon. But the gist of the matter can be told in few words.

1. Jesus worked from within outwards. He worked upon individual hearts to begin with. He aimed at reconciling men to divine order. He bade them take upon themselves, in penitence and lowliness, the yoke which they had in impatience cast away—the yoke of God's authoritative law. Till each single soul, drawn by love, had cast away its wilfulness and pride to return beneath the sway of the heavenly Father as a meek, forgiven, willing son of God, subject to the control of eternal law, Jesus counted nothing done at all; nothing radical, nothing effectual, nothing permanent. Not that He did not pity the fleeced peasantry of Galilee, ground down with taxation, or deplore the innumerable confusions and wrongs of His unhappy country. But in political remedies for all that—men being what they were—He appears to have had no faith; in remedies of violence, probably less than none, seeing these only intensify the deeper mischiefs they are meant to cure. A return to individual rightness, which implies the setting up within each microcosm of a human heart the rule of God's own righteous and loving will—this is a remedy that in the end-result must cure all ills.

It may seem slow, but it is sure. For it is not so much men's circumstances which want changing, as men themselves. Once made right, they will rectify their surroundings in due time. But no conceivable change of political position or social advantages can bring more than superficial help to a man who remains the slave of his own ungoverned passions and the enemy of God.

The end toward which Jesus worked was thus quite different from that of the insurgents and malcontents and would-be Christs of His time. It was a brotherhood of individuals turned from their sin, and so new-made in a religious sense; obedient each of them in his own conscience to the supreme law of holiness, and therefore constituting in the aggregate a spiritual kingdom of God. It is just as certain that this is not what the most advanced secular reformers of our own day are driving at. They too desiderate a regenerated society. They too cry after a brotherhood of men. But it is not within each man's soul and conscience that their movement takes its rise. They do not inculcate private repentance to begin with, or reconciliation to the rule of God, or the subjection of the passions to divine command. The social changes which they expect are not at all to be conditioned by individual holiness; and the ideal kingdom after which they are in pursuit will not prove to be, when it comes, a kingdom of God. An ideal does unquestionably shine before the eyes of enthusiasts in plenty; and that speaks well for the moral earnestness of our century, an earnestness which deepens as the century nears its close. Only the ideal is of a republic of men, not of a kingdom of God; a social commonwealth from which injustice is to be expelled, and penury, and oppression, and excess, and discontent, and every form of human evil, while yet it furnishes no method at all for banishing any one of these evils from the bosom of a single human being! Vain dream! That society can be better than the elements which compose it! That a kingdom of saints can be realized when you have made no man a saint to be its subject, nor set up over it any Lord of saints to be its King!

2. Such difference as there is in the ends pursued by Jesus and Barabbas respectively, such is there likewise in their methods. The method of Barabbas was simple enough—insurrection, robbery, and murder. When the rude demand in the popular breast for a new social order breaks out, it can only oppose violence to violence, and selfish passion to selfish passion—the selfish vengeance of the many against the selfish pride and tyranny of the few. But crime is not a remedy against wrong. At best it can only substitute one evil for another. No millennium can be built upon injustice, or even upon force. Appeals addressed to the private interests or to the unbridled desires of unregenerate human nature do nothing to regenerate that nature itself. If you would reach Christ's goal, you must follow Christ's method. First reconcile man to God, then man to his fellow. Bring men one by one to submit to the law of God, which is a law of righteousness and of love. Make them alike the children of a heavenly Parent. Do this by spiritual forces: by righteousness, that is, and by love. Be yourself a pattern, as Jesus was, of loyalty to principle that can die, but cannot sin against God; of disinterested devotion to the cause of others that will give its own life, not take the life of any. Barabbas robbed; Jesus toiled to serve and give. Barabbas was a murderer; Jesus laid down His life for us. Pride of self-assertion was the

key to the one character—pride that revolts against authority, divine as well as human, does evil that good may come, and wars against wrong in its own naked strength, as the wild beasts do—tooth and claw. Lowly love is the key to the other—love that respects before all things the law of God and the rights of man, is first just, then pitiful, and counts not its own life dear unto it, that it may save from death the children of the needy. Which will you have? Between these two ideals, between these two methods, every nation must at one time or another make its election. England may have to make it before long. When the people of any land in East or West are mad enough to cry—and mean it—" Not this Man Jesus, but Barabbas," the ruin of that land is near.

These things come closer home to us as individuals than some of you may think. Have we lost faith, like the Jewish priests, in a kingdom of God? Are we content to let the world's evils alone if only they let us alone? Satisfied if only we can gain or keep what will serve our turn? More solicitous for our private well-being than for the general weal or our neighbours' salvation? That at least is not Christianity. Christianity, whatever it is, is not a selfish religion. And he who has never learnt to look beyond his personal or material interests; still more, he who is ready to barter at any moment the whole cause of Christ and the kingdom of God, to save his purse or his ease and position; he does not yet know what following Christ means. There is a practical secularism which counts more converts than the theoretical. You may never say it, but you may live the saying: "We have no king but Cæsar."

But if we are interested in the progress of our species, the welfare of our fellow-men, or the bettering of society, are we following Christ's method to Christ's ideal kingdom? For instance: have you begun at home? The kingdom of God is first "within you." Is it true that you have come to God by Christ, a penitent confessing disloyalty, accepting pardon, and enthroning His blessed will as law over your own affections, motives, and pursuits? Is the mind of God, disclosed in Jesus' life, the regulative thought with which you strive to bring yourself into harmony? Then you cannot live for yourself. You must be making a little kingdom of God close by you, among your own nearest, at home, in your Church or neighbourhood—striving to bring other hearts under the sway of the same law of holy love. And you should be doing it in Jesus' spirit: with scrupulous care to do no wrong to any in the effort to do good; humbly serving the needs of others at your private cost; and by sweet gentleness, patient endurance, unwearied kindness, and faith that never faileth, winning hearts to the cross of the Son of God. To do this is to be loyal to Christ's mind. To do this—and be content to let the sacred spirit of love steal its slow and silent way from soul to soul, awaiting the issue God will send in a quiet trust that sooner or later His kingdom will come! Thus to live out Christ's life, and be in the world as He was, a leaven of God working in secret, is not easy. It is hard. It is unacknowledged, it is unrequited, on earth. It is a sacrifice of the very will and soul of one's self which no chaplet crowns and no crowds applaud. But it is loyalty to the Divine Man and Master: and that pays all! It is drinking out of His cup Whom the people refused. It is such work as only the humble can do, and the believing, and the patient, and the unselfish, and the pure of heart; and because it asks for such graces of the Spirit, it hath its reward of God—a reward that overpays all loss, and in the end shall weigh down meek brows that wear thorns to-day with a crown of glory which fadeth not away!

THE GENTLENESS OF CHRIST'S METHOD.

SERMON X.

THE GENTLENESS OF CHRIST'S METHOD.

"He shall not strive, nor cry; neither shall any man hear His voice in the streets. A bruised reed shall He not break, and smoking flax shall He not quench."—ST. MATT. xii. 19, 20, quoting ISA. xlii. 2, 3.

DURING that singular period in the recorded adventures of King David when he was an outlaw, he gathered around him, as we are told, a band of desperate and "broken" men. "Mighty men of valour" they were, tales of whose prowess lingered long in the traditions of Israel; their exploits of daring sung in ballads, and their skill in the use of manly weapons deemed worth recounting in the grave annals of revelation. Among such men it would not occur to any one to look for gentleness. Rough stalwart heroes, half patriot and half bandit, lion-slayers and giant-slayers, it is not in their wild cavern that you expect to meet with delicate consideration or chivalrous forbearance.

Yet when you do happen upon a soul of exceptional elevation, you find that strength and courage are quite capable of allying themselves with a tenderness almost feminine. At the head of these same freebooters, laying a strange spell even upon them, was a man at whose lightest word they would rush gladly to meet death, and the lifting of whose finger was enough to check their violence. The David of Israel's traditions, the hero of its war of independence, the mightiest among its fierce champions, was a man with a woman's gentleness, displaying a soul as melting, a courtesy as chivalrous, and a forbearance as delicate, as ever breathed in human bosom.

It was one of those features in that remarkable man which made him, with all his faults, a fit mirror of the Christ to come. For if tenderness to the feeble or the vanquished be a sure mark of a nature that is unusually noble as well as powerful, then it must become Him Who to the infinite strength of Godhead unites the adorable nobleness of Godhead too. Strength is good; but strength consecrated to the work of mere destruction is not good. Far better is the tamed and bridled strength which, having abashed the proud and reduced the wilful, lends itself next to the service of mercy; which stoops its crest to console the vanquished, and bends its back to raise the fallen. To restore is more divine than to destroy. It asks no less of power; but it asks something as well which is more precious than power. To gather up what remains, to mend the broken and heal the injured, to nourish what is weak into vigour again, and fan the expiring flame of life by gentle breath,—this is the work of a Saviour, of a Healer.

In its moral features, therefore, our Lord's task among men allies itself to those features of the divine operation in nature which are most God-like. Think how the unwearied agency of physical life on the globe is for ever at work, by slow and patient steps labouring to repair waste, and foster growth, and fashion new forms out of decay, and train young creatures to maturity, and in a thousand ways to renew continually the face of the earth. Just so does

THE GENTLENESS OF CHRIST'S METHOD. 133

Christ go to work. His mission was to save. He came to upbuild our ruined race; to spare what remained from man's original goodness; to evoke and develop the capability of growing better. In Him was strength, but it was strength gently used; strength waiting upon the bidding of kindness; strength that was full of tenderness, and full of patience, and full of condescension. It was such strength as, in the words of this prophetic Scripture quoted by the historian of His ministry, would neither break off a bruised reed nor quench entirely the dimly burning lamp.

Possibly it may encourage some of us if we meditate for a little on this surprising gentleness in One so strong as the Son of God. Although our illustrations of it must be borrowed from the days of His earthly ministry, they are none the less applicable to Him with Whom you and I have now to do, since He is "the same yesterday, and to-day, and for ever."

The points I shall invite you to notice will be these—

1. The unobtrusive, silent, and patient methods which our Lord employs in His work.

2. The use He condescends to make of the least remnant or commencement of good in a man. And—

3. The tenderness which He exhibits to those who have suffered from the storms of this life.

First, St. Matthew found himself reminded of this passage in Isaiah when he beheld how our Lord shrank from strife, almost from notoriety, declining to avail Himself of agencies which were obtrusive or vulgar, and preferring to carry on His mission in the most quiet and gradual method. Such a method is in accordance with the temper described in the text. Reeds half broken by the wind are to be met with in lonely spots. The household lamp of which the wick burns dim for failing oil belongs to the care of a quiet housewife. Both images speak, therefore, of work done in privacy. They found a striking commentary when our blessed Lord, evading those shouting crowds in Galilee and charging the multitudes not to make Him known, withdrew to solitary hills on the outskirts of the land, close to the borders of Phœnicia, there to bind up the broken heart of a woman of Canaan, and fan the feeble faith of His followers into such a flame as should by-and-by illumine every land.

It is characteristic of genuine Christian work that it puts no confidence in cheaply won success. You may stir widely the surface of society by means of advertising yourself; by blare of trumpet and windy contests with adverse opinion; by the arts of the demagogue or of the agitator. But it is, after all, the surface of society you have stirred, and as a rule nothing more. Not with such "observation" nor by such arts does the kingdom of God usually appear. It is within us; in the heart and in the home. As stricken deer forsake the herd, so wounded consciences hide their smart. Genuine piety detests display and will not wear its heart upon its sleeve. Little, therefore, is gained for the higher life by loud wrangling or street triumphs. Do not be disappointed because religion makes less stir in the world than politics or war. Do not grow impatient if little apparent outcome result from the preaching of the gospel. Do not conclude that Christ is not here because His voice is not heard in the market-place. The true annals of the Church are hidden, and the best work of the Church is done quietly. Quiet words in the obscure chapel; quiet petitions in the little prayer-meeting; quiet sobs in the lonely closet; quiet struggles in the silent heart; quiet victories over secret sins; quiet submission in the still death-chamber: by such methods and in such retreats does our great Lord carry forward the deepest and most permanent of all works done upon this earth—the work which shall endure, and have its everlasting monument in the hosts of the purified above.

Next, it is very encouraging to see how the Saviour does not despise, but is fain to use and to foster, the faintest elements of good in a man.

Take, for example, those of whom the crushed reed may stand for a fair emblem—persons who are so bent and broken under a sense of guilt, or of failure, or of moral worthlessness that they cannot hold themselves erect before Heaven. If in any condition a soul needs tender handling, being ready quite to sink and fail if roughly touched, it is when thus crushed by a sense of sin. How does Jesus deal with it? Take the instance of the fallen woman who threw herself in tears on His naked feet, and lay there sobbing. Think how forbearing He was to her; how profoundly sympathetic; how generous to defend her; how grand in His consolation—"Thy sins are forgiven! Thy faith hath saved thee! Go in peace!" Or take a case in which long habits of evil have corroded away whatever was once promising in the religious life, till one finds it hard to touch any chord that will reply, or to reach any remnant of faith in the Unseen beneath the layers of worldliness that wrap the heart. Too readily do we conclude such a case to be hopeless. Christ catches at the feeblest glimmer remaining. He reminds me of a skilful doctor hanging over one who seems drowned, flung ashore by the cruel tide; eager to hope against hope if he may revive what spark of vitality survives. Or like the woman who will not believe her lamp is gone out so long as it does but smoke, but fans it with soft and patient breath. Recall how He dealt with that thoughtless, loose-living woman of Sychar. How He tried one suggestion after another till He found the solitary article of her creed which had outlived a lascivious life—the solitary religious hope which smouldered within: "When Messias cometh, He will tell us all things." That was all that was left of her early religion, and on that He fastened, fostering the feeble faith into strength, till she became a glad witness for her Saviour and a missionary to her neighbours.

Surely there is something very divine as well as touching in this invincible faith of our Redeemer in the salvability of the men whom He came to save. It rebukes our too easy despair of the fallen. It reads us a lesson of hopefulness and of perseverance. It tells us that no man is so far gone but he retains something which may yet revive and lead him on to better things. Some soft spot is left in the hardest heart. By some avenue may compunction and relenting reach the most obdurate conscience. Some sweet memory lives yet; some pure affection in the roughest nature will be ready to leap to the light, like a spring of water, could you but tap it. What skill is required, what patient faith, what sympathy, and what gentleness, in One Who would be a Saviour for all men!

On the other hand, here is encouragement for those who judge themselves most hardly. Here is not One Who will strike you because you are down, or pass you by because you are unclean, or despair of you because you are well-nigh as bad as you can be! I warrant you, He is just the One to see some good about you where you yourself see none, and to toil on when other people give you up. It is well for some of us that He is less easily disheartened about us than we are ourselves. Let us pluck up courage, since our Saviour does not bate a jot of His brave hopefulness. Had you never seen a spring-tide, you would not have believed the black branches could put forth a tender green again; you would have despaired of the tiny seed ever piercing the frozen walls of its grave to revisit the light of upper air. Ah, God has surprising faith. It is faith in Himself and in that voice of His which bids dead things live and breathe again in the yearly resurrection. So hath our Lord Jesus a surprising faith in His own power to save. Do you say, "We are cut off for our parts; our bones are dried; our hope is lost"? Do you feel so long used to irreligion, so incapable of ever being pious, so dead at heart, so destitute even of a desire to do well, that you are like a withered thing, worthless and castaway? He never casts away. In that very sense which you retain of your own spiritual deadness, He reads a possibility of life. Slight may the possibility be, it is enough for Him. Wisely cherished, it will grow. He binds up the character that hangs by a thread. He breathes on the lamp that glimmers and smokes in act to expire. God help us if we had not such a Saviour, Who is hopeful to the last and patient with the worst, making the most of the least, of the things that remain and are ready to die!

There is yet another use which may be made of the same feature in the character and work of Christ—a use encouraging to a different class. Good people are often painfully weak in their goodness. They cannot say but they have some wish to be holy and to do good, yet all they do is like nothing at all—it is so little. Therefore they are always of a tremble within lest they be no Christians after all; shivering disciples who never feel sure enough of themselves to be of use to any other. It is certainly extremely disheartening to harbour this suspicion, that one is not enough of a Christian to be of the least use. Too little secure of one's own footing to hold out the hand to a brother. Too timid, or too faithless, or too poor in gifts and cleverness to be a working, helpful member in the body of Christ. Is there any ground for such feelings, then? I think not. Our Lord is not so fond of great things as to despise in this way the small things. He is not so much of a friend to John as to neglect the doubts of Thomas. He is far from overlooking the widow's mites because rich men are casting in of their abundance. He is like the woman who will not lose a penny-piece for want of a thorough search, nor let a wick expire for lack of fresh oil. The least is precious; the crumbs are to be gathered up. With a Friend of such a temper and of such habits, do not despond because you are feeble and poor in grace. In the world of labour there are cases in which willing hands are left unemployed because all they could do at their best would not pay for the trouble of teaching them. It is never so in Christ's workshop. He does not refuse, He begs for, the assistance of the least; and if it be for the backwardness of your religious life that you cannot do more, have patience; He giveth more grace. I think we are apt to be overhasty both with ourselves and others. We think everybody ought to become very good all at once. As well expect little children to grow quite wise in a week. In all God's work progress is slow. There is no hurry about Him to Whom a thousand years are as one day. Let us not hastily conclude that there is no good in us because there is less than we should like, or no use for us because we are less useful than somebody else. If the patient Lord knows we are as feeble as a reed, even a crushed reed, He will not lay on us a weight in excess of our strength. Yet He means to make good use of us one day for all that. The day comes when the frail and bending reed shall be "a pillar in the temple of our God." So of your flickering religious faith; a spark scarce kindled; a lamp so dimly burning that it lights no one. But He is too wise to cover it over with a bushel. He will gently fan; He will screen and shield you; He will secretly supply fresh oil from the reservoir of the Spirit's life. The time will come when the glimmering wick shall shine forth like the sun in the kingdom of your Father.

Finally, I should like to leave one closing word of cheer with those of us who have come to grief in the storms of life. We cannot be always young and strong. Every one cannot be successful or happy. It is all very well so long as the pleasant weather lasts. Even feeble humble folk will flourish then. Beside the brook that babbles past a woman's cottage door, see how the flags and rushes toss their heads in glee as the soft breeze of evening plays over them, fetching a low sad music out of their whispers and their rustles; while just inside her door, when the sun is down, the widow lights her little lamp to make cheerful the brief summer night. But wait a few hours. A treacherous gust out of a leaden sky has rushed down the little valley. Behind it came the thunder rain; and when the night squall is past, the moon looks out on battered beds of sedge and reed. Each frail stem that swung so cheerily to the sunset lies cracked and flattened now, never to rise again; while inside the cottage door all is gloom, for the first gust proved fatal to the widow's taper, and the light of her dwelling is gone out in darkness.

Alas! what disasters darken the homes of men! What wreck overtakes their business or their fortune! When such things come, this world does seem a cruel, a relentless place. Each calamity leads on its fellow. Misfortunes never come single. The fallen find it hard to rise. The candle of prosperity is rarely relit. Society shows scant forbearance or tenderness to the unfortunate. For society is a mob that jostles and pushes for precedence, each one for himself. Once a man is down, it tramples on him. In its haste to succeed, or to worship success, the public has little leisure to spare for lives which need to be tended and cared for. The victims of this modern "struggle for existence" resemble the fugitives from a stricken battle-field, overborne and trodden down before the wild mad rush of the conquerors. I wonder if there are any such here—men of broken fortune, of broken health, of broken spirits, out of whose lustreless eye the gleam of hope and courage has faded quite. My brothers, let me tell you of One Who finds time to care for you. In the rear of the fight comes the Physician and the Priest of the unhappy; picks His slow way among the fallen; catches the groan of the forgotten; binds up the bruises of the wounded; hears the confessions of the dying. My brothers, it is Jesus. To Him the unfortunate are as welcome as ever. It is of old His favourite task to bind up the bruised heart, to rekindle hope in the fading eye. If you have failed in life; if you are grown old in labour; if the body is diseased, and the world unkind, and friends are few, and death is near, turn to Him Who never lays a too heavy finger on any broken heart.

His gentleness will revive the fainting spirit. He will speak of peace, and rest, and forgiveness, and hope, and heaven. He will promise comfort to the forsaken, and to the dying eternal life. "He will not break the bruised reed; He will not quench the smoking flax."

WATCHING BY THE CROSS.

SERMON XI.

WATCHING BY THE CROSS.

"They sat and watched Him there."—St. Matt. xxvii. 36 (R.V.).

Some of us have wandered along foreign highways till, at a place where two roads met, we came upon a gaunt and weather-beaten figure by the wayside, a poor, coarse figure as of One upon a cross; and before it in the dust we have seen the grey-haired peasant kneel on his way from daily toil, and the market-woman with her basket; for, to the careworn and weary hearts of these simple folk, that harsh, ungainly crucifix, blanched with sun and rain, spoke of a love that never grows old, and of a divine sorrow which makes God in heaven a fellow-sufferer with the meanest upon earth.

Surely we have a different and a better reminder. Our Lord has been at pains to secure that His crucifixion shall never fade away from memory nor be long absent from the thoughts of His people. The holy eucharistic rite is a monument set up by His own hand, which forces upon the attention of every one that awful event at Jerusalem. There for ever seems to hang in view of all ages the most mournful, yet most comforting, of earthly sights. It calls upon us, as we press forward on our road of life, dusty and wayworn, to stop and gaze, to ponder and to pray.

We are all too apt to be but heedless wayfarers. Absorbed in our business or our play, we need to have this sobering spectacle of love and pity thrust upon our frequent sight. For the cross will not discover its true inner meaning to careless observers. Not if you hurry past; not even if you look with unpurged eyes, or come to it in a cold mood, void of love. It asks for study, pains, and prayer. To a true watcher by it, the cross of Calvary is the one spot of light and consolation for our unhappy race. Yet with what different eyes is it regarded! With what different eyes did men actually gaze upon it on that spring day when the sun of Syria was eclipsed! Some were heedless and some were puzzled. To many even who loved Him well it seemed the saddest and strangest of all sights. Was there so much as one whom love and penitence had taught to pierce beneath the shame and sorrow of it to that mystery of glory which lay at its very heart?

Let us join ourselves in imagination to these watchers by the cross and see what it will say to us.

I.

Surely we shall all of us see more in the sight than did those four Roman soldiers, of whom St. Matthew tells us that "sitting down they watched Him there,"—more, and with other eyes from theirs. It was only with dry eyes and a languid professional interest that these foreigners could watch how the Jew would die. A welcome relief it had been from barrack routine, giving zest to the fatigue duty of the day, to bait with cruel mischief this inoffensive Hebrew and laugh over His ridiculous pretensions to be a king. Even that grew stale; and when they were tired of their sport and had settled the important matter of a fair division of His clothes, what remained to while away the tedious hours of execution but sit down and watch Him there?

II.

Too cold and rude were the hearts of those poor fellows who "knew not what they did," the coarse, unconscious tools with which Roman justice executed that day its bad work. With a little more insight and a little keener sympathy did their superior officer sit there and watch with them. The centurion in command was a foreigner likewise; but he had learnt enough in Judæan society about this so-called Prophet and Messiah to take more than a merely official interest in the proceedings. While he observed Him, too, the behaviour of the Man awed him by degrees into respect, and stirred in his mind a wonder who or what He might be. Let us look for a moment through his eyes.

To such end has come so good a life! A kind and brave and gentle-hearted Man is this, even if He is no more. Only yesterday He was the darling of the populace, for He spent His blameless life in going about among them doing good. It was because He stood up for the common people that the rabbis detested Him. Where are all His Galilean supporters now, and the crowds who shouted "Hosanna!" a week ago? Are there none here of the numerous sick whom He is said to have cured? None whose friends He restored to reason or raised from the dead? Why is He hanging there, forsaken, to die? Such is the fate of your reformer and philanthropist. A victim, on the one hand, to the jealousy of the privileged orders whom He had the courage to assail; a victim, on the other hand, to the fickle ingratitude of the public whom he befriended! It is always the way. Yes, but see how strangely this Man takes it! All the morning He has not made one effort to rally His adherents. He has not uttered a single sound in protest, remonstrance, or complaint. Nay, He has not even exhibited any emotion of surprise, of indignation, or of disappointment. How is this? Does He know there is no chance of a reaction in His favour? Even then what self-control is required to take it all so passively! Is this stoicism? Or is it magnanimity? Surely His silent fortitude is sublime. His endurance and nobility of spirit are more than human. He bears His misfortunes, this Man, like a god!

III.

So far only was it possible for this intelligent watcher to go, since He stood outside the circle of Hebrew belief and knowledge. Some were watching there, however, who had come a good deal closer to the mysterious Sufferer and seen a good deal more of Him. There were many Jews who had followed His whole career from the beginning with profound interest—not without a hope, more or less decided, that He might turn out to be the long-looked-for Deliverer. He seemed in many ways to stand far above the vulgar pseudo-Messiahs of the time. He struck such a lofty note. He lived so pure and elevated a life. His teaching was so pregnant. His manners were so simple and unworldly. There sat upon Him so meek a majesty; yet withal He advanced such astounding claims, and sustained them with deeds of unquestionable power. All this bred in a widening circle of thoughtful and sincere Hebrews the hope that "a Prophet thus mighty in deed and word before God and all the people" was really "He Who should redeem Israel!" Men of this temper watched Him die with a dumb sickening sense of despair. It was not simply one more disappointment of the long-deferred hope. It was worse. It seemed to paralyze one's faith both in God and in human nature, that such a man as Jesus of Nazareth should turn out but a vulgar impostor after all! Was that possible? If not, how explain this closing scene? Does God abandon a genuine Messiah in His need? Did He raise our hopes only to dash them? If such a wonder-working Prophet as this cannot save His own life, dare we ever look for any real Saviour or Deliverer again? Then is Israel forsaken indeed, if her God has forsaken her!

IV.

There must have been many in Israel that day, private and obscure hangers-on of the Crucified, who (like the two at Emmaus) could do no more than start these questions of despair. Could His apostles not answer them? Such men as the Evangelist Matthew, for example; men who shared His most private hours, down even till this morning; men who were close by His side during last evening's supper and in the midnight retreat where they arrested Him: do they not know that their Master could defend Himself if He chose? Let them tell us, as together we watch Him die, what they know. Surely again and again has Jesus spoken of His approaching death as inevitable and yet as part and parcel of His career as Messiah.[1] Only last night He foretold in the upper room His betrayal, desertion, and capture as it came to pass. When they took Him, Matthew heard Him with his own ears say, "Thinkest thou that I

---

[1] See Matt. xvii. 22; xx. 17, 28; xxvi. 12.

cannot beseech My Father, and He shall even now send Me more than twelve legions of angels? How then should the Scriptures be fulfilled, that thus it must be?"[1] This man goes to His fate, it is plain, with His hands self-tied, of His own free will. He would not let a sword be drawn in His defence. He would not pray a prayer for celestial succour. Before His judges He would not say one word to bespeak their clemency. There was no bating of His awful pretensions; for before the Sanhedrim He accepted this morning the title of "Messiah, Son of God," and added, "I say unto you, Henceforth ye shall see the Son of man sitting at the right hand of power, and coming on the clouds of heaven."[2] There was then no decay of confidence in His own divine origin and spiritual office and superhuman authority; but there was a most deliberate, persistent declinature to avail Himself of any means of deliverance; a resolute yielding up of Himself to suffer everything which His enemies chose to inflict. He spoke like a man in the hands of destiny. "The hour," He said, "had come," and He went submissively to meet His fate. It was not that He could not have saved Himself, but quite clearly that He would not try.

We, therefore, as we sit now and watch Him on the cross, can understand better than the centurion that remarkable silence and composure of His. It is not pride refusing to own defeat: for He is not in reality defeated. It is more than magnanimity under misfortune: for the misfortune is of His own choosing. While His enemies congratulate themselves that they have got their way at last, He can afford to be serene, for in truth they are working out as unconscious instruments the doom which He has anticipated,

---

[1] Matt. xxvi. 53, 54.   [2] Matt. xxvi. 63-66.

foretold, and prepared for from the first. For such a strange surrender of Himself to be put to death, Jesus must have strong reasons of His own. It does not follow that those who sit to watch Him die can understand His reasons. We have not found Him easy to understand. Did any one understand Him when of late He set His face steadfastly to go up from a safe retreat in Galilee to the perils of Jerusalem? How often has His conduct baffled His best friends! As when Peter, for example, ventured to remonstrate with Him on His anticipation of this bloody tragedy, " That be far from Thee, Lord!" With this mysterious Man it is ever the unexpected that happens. Who expected to see Him hang like that—naked and dying on a cross? Who knows what He means by it?

V.

If any one of the select band of His intimates might be expected to read their Master's secret heart, it was surely John, the favourite and most intimate of them all. John is watching here at the cross foot while the heavy hours go past. One wonders what he sees in it all. Perhaps from his memoirs of the event something may be gathered. John was personally acquainted with the high priest, and had access to official sources of information. He knew the theory on which Caiaphas in secret council had advised the government to sacrifice Jesus.[1] It had been put as a patriotic duty to offer a single life as a victim to the suspicion of the Roman overlord rather than, by letting the movement go too far, provoke their foreign masters to destroy Hebrew nationality altogether. Can it be that Jesus Himself sympathizes with this view of the situation?

---

[1] John xviii. 16; xi. 47-53.

Is He patriot enough to accept the *rôle* of a victim to imperialism? Scarcely. John knows well enough that his Master's claims constituted no real political danger. That very day John had watched most narrowly the painful and prolonged efforts of the Roman governor to save his Prisoner. No! the Roman feared nothing, and had nothing to fear, from a shadowy kingdom which abjured the power of the sword. The plea of Caiaphas was merely a pretext on the part of that wily pontiff to disguise his real spite against the Prophet of Galilee.

For all that, had not John heard his dear Master use language which bore a startling resemblance to the suggestion of Caiaphas? Did He not speak once, some months ago in a corridor of the Temple, about Himself as a Shepherd of Israel Who, instead of fleecing the people like false rulers, meant to offer His own life to the wolf that the scattered children of God might be collected and kept in safety? What is more singular still, He spoke then of His self-sacrifice as actually a duty which He owed to God, and a free-will act of His own doing.[1] Other dark utterances of similar import rise likewise to recollection. In that memorable Capernaum sermon, for example, about the manna, just a year ago, how He scandalized the people by speaking of His own flesh and blood as given to be eaten for the world's life![2] That was a hard saying at the time: may it not shed some light upon this cross now? Nay, when one thinks of it, did He not use the very same language, no further gone than last night, at the Passover supper? All His talk then was to comfort us, because He was going away: how little we thought it was in this awful manner He was to be taken from us! Yet He told us

---

[1] John x. 11-18.   [2] John vi. 51-58.

plainly while He broke the loaf it was thus His flesh was to be rent; and see how His dark blood like wine is flowing now! How, then, did He explain the meaning of this deliberate and bloody close to His career? Did He not say His body was to be broken *for us*, and His blood shed for the *remission of our sins?* Did He not invite us to feed upon Him after death? Ah, then, He is Himself a true Paschal Lamb, an innocent Victim slain for the errors of the people! And the meaning of His willing self-oblation must be that He perceives He cannot otherwise propitiate for the sins of His followers or give to them eternal life.

In the dawn of his own spiritual history, St. John had been a penitent scholar of the great Baptist. In the vast laver of the Jordan he had sought to cleanse his conscience with a cleansing which it could not give him. And the words which first sent him after Jesus of Nazareth had been these great words, "Behold the Lamb of God! He beareth away the sin of the world."[1] How was it that these words never disclosed their full significance—never until now? A God's Lamb verily, for sweet guilelessness and stainless innocence and incomparable meekness—oh, how the beauty of this Man's character had from the first endeared Him to the heart of John! But a Lamb that bears sin to bear it away must be a sacrifice, slaughtered because unblemished, meek and dumb in death, a victim for the priests to offer! And see! how silently He hangeth there, supreme in patience, a bleeding Lamb indeed! Ah, priest Caiaphas! how much more do thy words mean than thou meanest! This holy lamb-like Victim Whom thou and thy fellow-priests are offering up to political necessity or to class rancour, is self-offered in a far holier cause! Not to save Judæan

[1] John i. 29-37.

nationality, but to propitiate for the sin of the whole world. Yes, here is a key, the only one that will unlock the riddle. Say that He gives His pure life to God, a spontaneous Victim for the guilt of His people, how significant become then the attendant circumstances! It will account for His strange passivity and silence; for (as Isaiah wrote long ago), "He is led like a lamb to slaughter; and, as a sheep before her shearers is dumb," so, in token of meek consent, Jesus "opens not His mouth." This explains, too, why He refused to beg for celestial cohorts to rescue Him; for, as He said Himself, "to lay down His life is a commandment He received from His Father." See, ah, see, how the centurion thrusts into His heart the cruel lance! Is it not written, "They shall look on Me Whom they pierced"? No; *His* limbs the soldiers will not dare to break when they break the others; for how reads the law of the Passover lamb? "A bone of him shall not be broken."[1]

Thus, through that anointing which teacheth all things, we may judge it possible for John the theologian, as with breaking heart he watched beneath his Friend's cross, to penetrate a little way into the great mystery of expiation, and learn how, as he wrote afterwards to the Church, the Son of God was manifested to bear sins by making His life a propitiation for them, that His blood might cleanse us from all unrighteousness.[2]

VI.

Let us not forget that close by the side of the beloved theologian there stood the women who loved Him best. Some tender hearts, few but tender, of the mother who

---

[1] John xix. 31-37.
[2] 1 John iii. 5 (margin of R.V.), with i. 7 to ii. 2.

bore Him, and the matrons who tended Him, and the saved and healed who owed Him more than life: how these stood and watched Him as He died! Not with questions of theology were their thoughts full that day, not with the "how" and "why" of His strange sacrifice; but they were filled with the sorrow of it—filled with the pity of it! Why their Beloved needed to be so cruelly handled, or the redemption of their souls had to cost a life so precious, it was not theirs to ask! God only knows and He Who suffers it. But that He bears it all for our poor sake, and for the mighty love He has to us, and that He has not deserved one least pang of it all—not one; but we have deserved it, and He bears it for us: *that* at least our simple hearts may know, and at the thought a sword does pierce our own souls also! Oh, it was so good of Him! What infinite kindness made Him stoop to bear all this for us? How meek and willing He hangeth there! How the nails tear His flesh! How the death-darkness sits upon His brow! How pale His face, where the blood scores red lines! And He so good, so spotless, so patient, and so holy! Oh, the sorrow of it! Oh, the love and pity of it!

He always used to tell us His Father in heaven loved us; and this, though we did not know it, was to be the measure of that love! Ah! He knew God's heart, for He lived with God; and He said it was a Father's heart that yearned after all men, just as He did Himself; and in His Father's name He used to promise pardon to the worst of men when they were sorry. To think that He had to come to this, to win such pardon for us!

For us! Are we, too, watching with Him here to-day, as the women did and John, beside His cross? Can we look through this touching story and meet His eye as they did? Do I know that He singles me out in my sin, and loves me in it, and died to save me from it? Oh, undecaying love of God, Who died for all! Oh, precious blood that cleanseth all! Oh, heart of mine, that canst be cold to One Who died for thee! What sorrow, that ever I have grieved my Lord! What contrition, what regret, become me for those hateful and ungoverned passions, those mean delights, those peevish or bitter tempers of my soul, which pierced the Saviour and which still are harboured within my breast! My God, Who didst come down to give Thy life for me, have mercy now at last upon this hard, blind, stony heart, and, ere it be too late, subdue, and melt, and win, and cleanse me for Thyself. Then will I too sit, and watch, and weep, and pray; and with an eye no less intent nor heart less penitent than the dying thief's, will say, "In life and death, O Lord, my Lord, remember me!"

UNTO ME.

SERMON XII.

UNTO ME.

A Sermon for Hospital Sunday.

"The King shall answer and say unto them, Verily I say unto you, Inasmuch as ye have done it unto one of the least of these My brethren, ye have done it unto Me."—St. Matt. xxv. 40.

About four days before these words were spoken, one of our Lord's adherents had attempted to set up a rivalry betwixt the claims of his Master and those of the poor. When a warm-hearted woman, moved with gratitude, broke over the feet of Jesus a costly vase of aromatics, Judas thought that a better use would have been found for the money had it been given in charity.[1] It was then, and it still is, a false sentiment which grudges the lavish offerings of piety to the honour of the Most High, or would make competing claims out of what is due to His worship on the one hand and to the service of suffering humanity on the other. Such an unseemly competition has no existence. The devout who spend most freely on religious objects are also as a rule the generous who give most largely to charity; whereas the man who is mean and niggardly to his Saviour will generally be found to stint his benefactions in a like degree. But if it were otherwise; if these two claims ever did enter into competition, so that

[1] Mark xiv. 3-9; John xii. 1-8.

we had to choose whether we should starve the needy for the adornment of a church or spare our offerings to Heaven that we might feed Heaven's poor; then our Lord has left us in no doubt which alternative will please Him the better. Edward Irving caused it to be engraved on the silver plate of his London church, that when the offerings of the people no longer sufficed for the wants of God's poor, the sacred vessels were to be melted down to supply the deficiency. He was right. It is the Master's mind. Christ has expressly transferred to the honest and suffering poor His own claim on the devotion of His people. Even while He was warmly defending the action of Mary of Bethany on that Saturday evening, He hinted that after He was taken away from the reach of our personal homage the poor would remain with us in His stead. He made this still more plain on the following Wednesday. When, in the majestic passage before us, He foretold with dramatic vividness the awful transactions of the judgment, He made it for ever unmistakable that the enthusiastic love of the Church for her absent and inaccessible Lord is now to pour itself out in deeds of practical beneficence, finding in the distressed a substitute for Him Who was once the Man of sorrows.

The lesson of our text is plain, then: the suffering are to us in the room of Christ. We cannot spend our treasures as Mary did in ministering to the personal honour or refreshment of our Divine Lord. He is far withdrawn now beyond need or reach of human ministry into the serene heaven of His glory. But, though absent, He has left His proxies behind Him. No disciple may excuse himself to-day from imitating Mary's open-handed gratitude on the plea that the Saviour is out of reach. For every purpose of devotion—for giving Him pleasure, for testifying our own thanks, for winning in the end His praise—it is really all the same if we minister to His poor ones as if we spent our money on Himself. Through this appointed channel is our homage to reach Him there, where, priest-like, He stands at the heart of this ailing race, a sharer in each man's sorrow. Be kind to His afflicted members: you have gratified Him as surely as though you could pour your tribute of devotion on His uplifted, crowned head. Withhold your kindness, and He will resent your selfishness as much as if He had been the suppliant you refused to help.

It is a most interesting question, Why does Christ thus find His true representatives in those who suffer? It is not a question very easy to answer. Naturally one recollects how Christ dwells in a special manner in His own people. With all godly persons who suffer He is closely identified, since He is the Head of His body, the Church; and if He meant the words "My brethren" to be strictly confined to the pious, we should not need to inquire further. But I am not satisfied that we can limit His words so narrowly. Are we to ask always, "Is this poor creature a Christian?" before we feel free to relieve him for Christ's sake? Or does Christ not care to reward your kindness to the undeserving? May I not minister to Him in every genuine case of distress, apart altogether from the religious character of the sufferer? These considerations are too strong to be overlooked. It must be on some other ground than their Christian faith that the Son of man makes common cause with the unfortunate. What reason has He for identifying Himself in some sort with every afflicted human being, or with human beings most when they are in affliction?

Was it because He chose to be Himself a Sufferer, poor, and acquainted with grief? The recollection of His own straitened lot and heavy trials may well predispose Him to care most for the unfortunate. An experienced and pitiful Saviour will naturally be drawn into closest sympathy with those whose case appeals most powerfully to His compassion, calls most loudly for His aid, or reminds Him most touchingly of His own past. But, in saying this, we merely touch the surface of the matter. Why was Christ's lot on earth cast among the humble and afflicted?

We must go down a little deeper and say, Our Saviour's design in coming here at all was to be a Healer, Rescuer, and Comforter for mankind. To One Who came forth from the unseen world of bliss on such an errand, the most suitable place and the most attractive would be the place where He was needed most. In His own language, the Physician must go where the sick are to be found; and the sore sad sickness under which humanity pines away to death is at once sin and the suffering which is sin's shadow. To get near enough to our stricken race that He might probe and know its misery, feel and bear its evil, and win the power at once to stanch its wounds and lift from it its whole burden, Jesus needed to become familiar with men in whom the malady had worked itself out to its painfullest consequences. Therefore "He bare our sicknesses and carried our sorrows." He became the companion of the unhappy, and the resort of outcast men and fallen women and the desperately sick whom no one else could save. It was on the shady side of life that He expected to find a welcome. The proud and prosperous are too well satisfied with the world and with themselves to make likely patients for a Divine Healer. Where people had drunk life's cup down to the bitter lees, and found at the bottom only failure, penury, sickness, and sorrow of heart, there He hoped to win a hearing for His soft and soothing call, " I will give you rest."

Still, I question if we are got to the root of this affinity betwixt the Saviour and the afflicted. It is true that He shared by preference the lot of the sad and broken in spirit that He might sound the depths of our great need and be able to speak to the heart when it is most disposed to listen. For all that, is He not the Son of man, Brother to all men, and Friend to whatever is best in human life—to its joys as well as to its griefs? Is it not for man as man He is come to care, rather than for man as suffering merely? Yes, there is truth in that. Only, when you come to think of it, is not this also true, that in this selfish and artificial world, the one thing which most swiftly and surely reveals the genuine humanity in every human being and brings all men together on a level, is suffering? Society is full of clefts which are very deep and yet are very unreal after all. So long as things go on gaily, men and women see merely the outsides of one another, and act towards each other a conventional part. The people you meet are either above you or below; some are employers to be served, and others labourers to be employed; you know them in business or you distinguish them in society by their several grades, professions, or style. Beneath all this that is artificial and conventional, where is, after all, the manhood and the womanhood which we all of us share in common as God made us? What is there which can discover *that* to us and make us feel it? What but our common afflictions? The presence of death makes the squalid hovel for the time like a sacred place. A mortal sorrow draws the palace into sympathy with the cottage. Every widespread disaster sends a thrill of emotion through all ranks among our people. The neighbour in whom at ordinary times you take no interest becomes an object of concern the moment some unusually tragic incident has crowned him with the sanctity of suffering. Oh, suffering has a wonderful power to emphasize our kinship! It makes you see no longer the pauper, the beggar, the obscure tradesman, or common labourer, but the *man*, your fellow, whose exceptional share in our common afflictions has lent him dignity and given him claims upon you which he never seemed to have before.

In this lies beyond doubt a great deal of the moral value of poverty and sickness. Society will never be able to rid itself of these; and, from a moral point of view, it would clearly be a pity if it could. For if all men were strong and happy and lucky and well-to-do, so that no one needed his fellow's assistance or addressed any call to his neighbour's compassion, what a world of selfishness would this grow to be, under the unchecked operation of economic laws—the laws of selfish competition and ambition! What a hard world! Every one feeling himself at liberty to push and thrust without scruple and without pity, with no feeble cry for mercy to evoke his sympathy, nor any wail of pain to melt him into tenderness. It is the presence among us of widows and orphaned babes; of faces hunger-pinched, and tortured bodies; of those who totter for tender years, and those who totter for helpless age; of the sick, and the maimed, and the fevered, and the wasting, and the dying;— it is this that never will suffer us, amid our rush after gain or pleasure, to forget that we too are *men*.

By bringing out in this way the underlying humanity

which makes us all kindred, does not misfortune bring out that in each of us which is next of kin to Jesus Christ? The Son of man is the Head of every man! How? Inasmuch as He too is a partaker in that which is common to us all. Not with people as social accidents have sorted them—as rich or poor, as wise or foolish, as lords and ladies or humble folk, has He that close affinity which makes Him call us all His "brethren;" but deep within these wrappings of rank or circumstance He Who shares our nature reads the characteristic features of our manhood—common infirmity, common need, common pains, and common mortality. In these it was that He took part. In these, as often as He sees them, He still claims to have a share. Whatever sharpens in your bosom the sense that your neighbour is your brother-man, must likewise sharpen the sense that he is a born brother to the Son of God. Is it not, then, due to this deep underlying unity of His nature with all our race, a race which, sundered by many things, is one in its sorrows, that Jesus Christ bids us discern Himself in every man who hungers, bleeds, weeps, or dies? With that most human of all things, suffering, the badge, not of a tribe, but of our whole race, has He most completely identified Himself, Who is Himself the Ideal Man and the Representative Sufferer for all mankind. *Ye did it unto Me!*

Whatever may be the grounds on which our Saviour has allied Himself with the unfortunate by bequeathing to them His own claim upon His people's kindness, it is clear, at all events, that His doing so has conferred at one stroke two great benefits: one benefit upon Christ's disciples, and another upon the poor and needy.

1. It has been a conspicuous blessing for Christ's people that when He went away He installed suffering humanity in His room, and bade them minister to it as to Himself. We must remember what a profound hold Jesus Christ took upon the heart of His followers, and how immense was the enthusiasm for Himself which He evoked. From the first century down till this latest one, Christ has drawn towards His own Person the most powerful and devoted attachment of unnumbered converts. His cross, by sounding every deep in the human soul, has subjugated the life of myriads and swept along in a tide of fervid devotion the grand currents of their hearts. Much more in some than others, but more or less in every one who fairly comes within its spell, the love of Christ has been and is the master-passion in Christian bosoms and the most effective as well as the most enduring of all enthusiasms known to history. Consider how great the misfortune would have been if Jesus had not yoked this gigantic force to the practical service of mankind. Had He cut no useful channel for it to run in, the current of Christian ardour and love for the departed Master could only have been wasted; or, like other misdirected religious enthusiasms, it must have spent its force in a mischievous asceticism or a more mischievous fanaticism. To a very serious extent, the forces of Christianity have been thus misspent. But that has been when Christian men forgot that their Master had set before them a task as gigantic as it is beneficent—the task of relieving human distress for His sake. Christ does not bid us fight in His cause; He forbids us to do that. He does not wish us to abjure society, and starve and macerate ourselves for His sake; He had rather we did not. He does not ask us to expend our main strength in

building cathedrals or chanting *Te Deums*, though we may lawfully do all that and much more in His honour. But if you would really like to please Him and manifest how thoroughly you appreciate and reciprocate His divine charity toward yourself, then He bids you feed the hungry, clothe the naked, and heal the sick. And if yours be a more than common heat of devotion, not to be satisfied with ordinary sacrifices or exertions, then there is no limit set to your philanthropy. You may sell all that you have and give to the poor. For the suffering are your Lord's residuary legatees; in them He is still to be found on earth; through their hands He will accept your gratitude. In doing them a service, ye do it unto Him.

2. If our Lord has done His Church a benefit by giving such a practical turn to her gratitude, how signal is the benefit which He has conferred on the afflicted members of our race! No such pregnant service was ever rendered to the cause of humanity. Right well did our Lord know that the claims of the unhappy require to be reinforced. Not that the appeal which misery addresses to the fortunate is one which has ever gone quite unheeded. Always some tender bosoms have been found to pity undeserved distress—some hands willing to assist it. But how few! how insufficient! Motives of humanity have never availed to conquer that selfish indifference to others which is the child of prosperity. Personal interest has proved to be too strong for compassion—too strong for the sense of duty to mankind. It was time that Jesus came to the succour of the neglected and forsaken with a reinforcement of prodigious strength. He made their cause His own. He sent forth the whole Church of His lovers and disciples to be one vast army of philanthropy. He laid every

sufferer as a burden upon the heart of Christians. To every one who calls Him "Lord" He flings out this challenge: Despise, forget these little ones, only if you dare forget and despise *Me!*

Are you astonished that He champions so magnificently the classes whom society is apt to hustle out of sight? I am not: but I will tell you what does surprise me. It surprises me exceedingly that the very classes whom He has taken under His wing and for whom He claims all that He might have claimed for Himself, are grown in a large measure to forget His grace and to despise His name! The destitute, degraded, and criminal classes in England have no such friend as Jesus Christ. If they have any friends on earth, they are chiefly such as Jesus sends them; gentle men and soft-spoken women who befriend them for Jesus' sake. If the homes of the poorest are visited in kindness; if dispensaries are open to give them physic; if hospitals receive them when helpless with wounds or fever; if the discharged prisoner is met with a welcome at the gaol door, and the homeless finds a refuge by night, and the orphan is tended and taught, and homes are created beyond the sea for the sons and daughters of callous parents; if, in brief, the hundred-handed charity of England is toiling day and night for the most useless and miserable portion of England's population, is it not due, four-fifths of it at the least, to the pity which Jesus Christ has quickened in men's breasts, and to the charge which He has left behind upon the conscience of all who love Him that they care for those His brethren even as for Himself? Yet among those He calls His brethren, how is Jesus Christ forgotten, His gospel scouted, and His name blasphemed!

If anything could neutralize the words of Jesus or cool

the hearts in which His heavenly love glows hot, I grant
you it would be when the objects of His kindness scorn our
holy religion, the very faith to which they and their children
owe so much; when they insolently claim as though they
had a right to it the undeserved mercy of Christian hearts;
or when they receive benefactions with a thanklessness
which traffics upon your goodness and knows no shame.
But, after all, this is true only of a portion; and were it more
generally true than it is, it could be no sufficient reason for
our ceasing to pity and to work for them, though it might
be a reason for our reconsidering the best way of seeking
their good. Charity will cover a multitude of sins; and
real patent, pitiable distress claims our help whether it
deserves it or not. Especially when sickness comes—such
sickness as drives poor people into the hospital—then the
most scrupulous may surely feel that charity is in its place.
It never can do harm to soothe pain or cure disease.
Although even medical charities, like every other human
thing, can be abused and sometimes are, yet on the whole
they are probably less liable to abuse than any other shape
of charity administered amongst us on a wide scale. For
them, therefore, I feel free to plead with confidence. It
is really our very Lord and Saviour Who pleads with us
to-day. As though He lay in the hospital ward and begged
at your hand for the cup of cold water or of generous wine,
so listen to the confused murmur of supplication which
reaches us from those innumerable homes of mercy where
skilful science lavishes its art, and patient nursing love
waits with deft and gentle hand, and all that skill and all that
love can do are done, not only for cheerful sufferers whom
Christ has taught meekly to bear His cross, not only for
the silent little children who lie so quietly in their cots and

make no moan, not only for the honest and deserving workman whose stricken strength has left the household cupboard bare at home and who cares less for his own ebbing life than for the thought of widowed wife and orphaned babe,—not only for these and thousands like them of the innocent, the gallant, or the upright whom adversity has smitten to the earth, but for the victims also of crime or of their own vile passions: for them also Christ pities, though they know Him not; and over them He would have our hearts bleed, seeing that in them too there dwells that ineffaceable human image of the Divine, which (in how changed a form) He Himself condescends to wear. Freely ye have received of Him, my brethren; to Him this day freely give—to Him in the person of these His brethren. "Inasmuch as ye have done it unto them, ye have done it *unto Me.*"

THE TWO HALVES OF CHRISTENDOM.

SERMON XIII.

THE TWO HALVES OF CHRISTENDOM.

"The kingdom of God is not meat and drink; but righteousness, and peace, and joy in the Holy Ghost. For he that in these things serveth Christ is acceptable to God, and approved of men."—ROM. xiv. 17, 18.

To an outside observer, Christendom offers the spectacle of a vast camp, split into two main divisions by widely differing theories respecting the nature of Christianity itself. The followers of Jesus have, indeed, separated into a great number of societies and sects. But, speaking broadly, these may all be said to group themselves under two banners according to the fundamental conception they entertain of the religion which He founded. On the one side stand shoulder to shoulder two immense societies, agreeing in their main views—the so-called Catholic Churches of the East and West, the Greek and the Latin communions. In spite of jealousies, these two great historical bodies possess a natural affinity for one another. They equally claim to derive by unbroken descent from the apostolic Church, and in their radical conception of salvation they are at one. Opposed to these two "Catholic" Churches, are ranged a crowd of smaller bodies: some of them in their existing shape three to four centuries old, and others much newer; some representing the faith of powerful nations, others boasting a mere handful of adherents; yet all agreed in the main upon a theory of Christianity which flatly contradicts the Catholic one. I have no wish to make too light of the distinctive tenets which divide Protestants, although I do not propose further to refer to them at present. We may at least take it for granted at the outset that the bulk of the non-Catholic Churches, however they may differ among themselves, are on the whole cut off from the Catholic ones by much deeper and wider differences. So that, as I said, Christendom is split in two by this main cleft. It is of their contrasted views on the way of salvation in general, rather than of their specific divergencies in teaching or practice, that I propose to speak.

At the same time, it is of consequence to recognize that this division, although a deep one, lies inside the Christian camp. It is not like the bounding exterior *fosse*, with ramparts, which guards the whole of the Christian enclosure and marks it off from the non-Christian or unbelieving world outside. In other words, Catholic and Protestant have far more in common with each other, after all, than either of them has with the antichristian beliefs or denials of belief which lie outside the pale of Christ's Church altogether. Although the points in controversy betwixt the Latin and the Reformed communions are of serious importance, they are not so important as the underlying doctrines of the Christian faith on which they are agreed. Wherein we differ shall presently be seen. Recall for a moment how far we are agreed upon most of the peculiar and vital dogmas of Christianity. We agree in holding that God has supernaturally revealed His will to mankind for our salvation, and that we possess in Holy Scripture the record of that revelation. We agree in worshipping the mysterious

Trinity of Persons within the Unity of the ever-blessed Godhead. We agree in believing that the Second Person assumed our human nature by His miraculous conception of the Virgin, and is for ever one mysterious Person in two natures, unconfounded and unchanged, yet joined in inseparable union. We agree in confessing the leading facts of Christ's saving work as our incarnate Redeemer—His sinless obedience, His vicarious expiating death, His resurrection, His ascension, and the coming of the Holy Ghost. We all equally regard His Passion as an atoning sacrifice offered for the sins of the world. We all equally believe in the perpetual presence of Christ in His Church through the invisible indwelling of the Holy Spirit. We all observe as valid means of grace the two sacraments of Baptism and the Lord's Supper. And we all look for our Lord's return to judge the world, for the resurrection of the dead, for the final punishment of the wicked, and for the everlasting felicity of the saints in heaven. On some of these great doctrines it may be that divergencies exist on minor details. On a few of them certain minor sects stand apart from the rest of Christendom. But so far as the central nucleus of Christian teaching and Christian believing are concerned, we have here a very large amount common to both Catholic and Protestant theology, and not shared by any who are not Christians. I cannot conceive what should make any person anxious to pare down to a minimum this *consensus* of Christendom. To my mind it is one of the most encouraging and hopeful of facts.

But our business just now is with the differences; and these stand in no need of exaggeration; they are sufficiently serious of themselves.

When I strive to penetrate to the bottom of this cleavage betwixt Christendom Catholic and Christendom Reformed, and ask myself where do their respective theories of our common religion diverge, I seem to get some such answer as this: The Catholic communions put in the foreground, as the main channel of God's mercy to mankind, the Society which Jesus founded. They make the Church the primary thing and the intermediate link between man's Saviour and each individual who needs salvation. According to this theory, what Christ did was to found a sacred Society and make it the depositary of Heaven's gracious influence, so that whoever keeps himself in orderly connection with that Society is sure of pardon and salvation, but no one else. Practically, therefore, what the individual has to do is to see that he is and remains a faithful son of his spiritual Mother the Church. He is referred at every turn of his religious experience to her officials. These officials are divinely constituted intermediaries betwixt him and Heaven. In their hands rests an ample apparatus of grace, of which they alone possess the monopoly. This apparatus of spiritual appliances covers the entire life of every Christian from his birth to his grave. Give yourself over into the care of Christ's privileged ministers, do as they tell you, employ faithfully their means of grace, and you will be led on from step to step of Christian life. You will be regenerated in baptism, anointed with the Spirit, disciplined or corrected when you go astray, fed with celestial nutriment in the Eucharist, and finally absolved and sealed for heaven on your death-bed. To be thus true to the ministry of the Church, her obedient, faithful son, is to be in a state of salvation. To forsake her pale or be expelled from it, is to be lost.

To this foursquare and very consistent theory, Protestantism offers another which is its direct contrary. According to Reformed Christendom, there is no such intermediary betwixt the Saviour and the sinner. The Christian Society cannot possibly hold any such place, because it does not in point of fact come first in order; it comes second. The first or initial fact was of old, and continues to be, an individual sinner, needy, criminal, and penitent, called to Jesus by His personal Word, and coming to Him by personal faith. Given any number of such persons uniting in their allegiance to Him, and you have the Church—a holy and helpful society, indeed, in which dwells the Spirit of its exalted Head, but not the indispensable channel of grace betwixt the Head and each member. In short, Protestant teaching begins by setting each man into immediate personal contact with the Lord Jesus Christ as the divine Object of faith, Source of life, and Guide of conduct. The officials of the Church it turns from intermediaries into helps; from priests, that is, into ministers. It insists upon it that salvation must hinge, not upon dutifully employing the Church's apparatus of grace, but on a direct approach of the soul to Christ in trust and obedient love. An immense train of consequences has, of course, been developed out of this radical difference of view, making the subject complex. But this is probably the starting-point of divergence, to which for the present we must confine ourselves.

Looking now at these two theories for the purpose of comparison, it strikes one that the difference lies less in the doctrines of Christ's religion than in the method by which His benefits are supposed to reach us. To the Catholic and to me alike Jesus our Lord remains the same Divine-human Person by Whose meritorious death we have been redeemed. To both the operation of the Divine Spirit is essential to salvation. Only we differ as to those human conditions which bring into one's soul the atoning virtue of the Saviour's death and the quickening power of the Spirit's life. These, the Catholic thinks, reach him through the hands of the one true Church and her officers. I think they reach me directly and at first hand, so soon as I approach the Saviour with penitence and faith.

Although the difference touches our creed far less than it does our experience, yet practically it is found to be a difference fraught with very serious results. It shifts the centre of gravity in the whole system. Each theory, therefore, generates a type of piety of its own. It colours the whole of Christian experience with its own complexion. Either theory, of course, may be run to an extreme, or it may be held in moderation. Those Christians who on either side are least pronounced in their views may approach one another pretty closely. Yet, even when good men of the two communions are most alike, it will be found that they look at things with different eyes in a thousand particulars, just because they have set out from opposite theories of Christianity.

Next, it cannot fail to strike you that between Churches holding such views, mutual toleration is impossible. I can tolerate the Roman or the Greek Catholic indeed, because, although I think he attaches far too much consequence to the Church, yet I have no doubt at all that he can, and often does, reach our Saviour through the Church. I may think he would reach Christ far better, more simply and more joyfully, by just going to Him at first hand, as we try to do. Still, I need not deny to our Lord either the power or the will to use His Church with her means of grace, and welcome to His saving mercy every honest, longing worshipper who comes to Him by that route. Therefore I can greet as my fellow-Christian every Catholic who loves our Lord in sincerity. Unhappily, he cannot do the same by me. For his theory has the misfortune to be an exclusive one. If the Church, with her sacraments dispensed by a duly descended ministry, be Christ's sole channel of grace, then to live outside her pale, still more to refuse her offices, means to live beyond the ordinary hope of salvation. This is an awkward conclusion for the Catholic Church. To be obliged to draw it must put her at a serious disadvantage. It binds her to be intolerant. She is forced to unchurch every non-Catholic communion; and she does it. Of course this isolates her in Christendom; and that isolation, which in other days, when she stood alone, added to her strength, must now, since she is girdled with rivals, increase her difficulties. To see a Church environed with purer Churches refusing to recognize them, nailing her colours to the mast as the sole bearer of salvation to mankind, and, if she be destined to sink amid the incredulity of modern Europe, prepared to go down with her ancient and haughty claim to a monopoly of truth and grace unlowered,—this is a strange sight, not without a pathetic and tragic dignity.

Another awkward result of the Catholic theory is that it appears to be contradicted by facts. It is very hard for the Catholic controversialist to deny that among Protestant bodies there have been found not a few most excellent specimens of the Christian graces—both men and women who, had they only happened to be born inside the true Church, would have been deservedly canonized as saints. To candid minds not biassed by controversy this looks like giving up the whole contention. If excellent Christians who wear the image of the Lord Jesus can be produced in crowds outside the Church, what becomes of her monopoly of grace? Are not the facts too strong for her theory? We who have been born and bred in the bosom of another communion and have lived in fellowship with its freer spiritual life, are perfectly well aware that Christian life flourishes outside all the so-called Catholic Churches. We know how true and sweet and manly is the piety which Protestantism can nurture; how Christ can be sought and found with no priest for a go-between; and how the most delicate flowers of devotion and the most heroic enterprises of Christian love will flourish in a soil which (on the Catholic theory) ought to be condemned to perpetual sterility. In the face of nearly four hundred years of such experience, it is impossible for us to believe that Christ gave to the Roman clergy or to any others a monopoly of the channels of salvation.

For a further reason, the step from the Protestant to the Catholic theory of salvation would be intellectually a step backward—a step, therefore, which, in spite of some splendid exceptions, few wise men will be ready to take. It is true that we have lost by the Reformation the power and fascination of a vast unbroken world-wide sacred and enduring organization. None of us, bred Protestants, can quite realize how much that means. It was an imposing dream that everywhere across Christendom there stretched one uniform, unchangeable society, Christ's own creation, empowered to lock or unlock the gates of heaven; within whose ample skirts every Christian soul could nestle, from the lowest to the highest; by whose gentle yet awful ministry all men might be rescued out of the kingdom of Satan, and made meet for the heaven of God. Men in their doubts crave for an authority to settle them. Distracted nations cry for some bond of brotherhood and unity. Feeble hearts long for a near visible strong arm to lean upon. Devotional natures seek for spiritual union with all pure souls everywhere. Here there is offered to us a home of all devotion, and a mother-bosom for every aching head, and a centre of spiritual unity for mankind, and an awful oracle which in God's name settles every difficulty. Yes, it is beautiful; a splendid dream, if one could only believe it. And this we have lost—for ever; because it never was more than a dream, and the Reformation shivered it.

In its room, what have we? We have a manlier faith: a faith which recognizes fully the awful gift of personal responsibility in man, elevates him to the dignity of immediate relationship with God, and links each solitary individual direct to heaven. Instead of overwhelming me beneath a vast society, the Evangelical theory asserts the lordship of Christ alone over my conscience, summons me to transact at first hand with God, sets me in the centre of a spiritual economy of salvation, the solemn forces of which play invisibly without ceasing upon my heart and will, and with which I am called to keep myself in living wholesome contact, nothing between. God, approaching me in the Incarnate, becomes the Only One I have to transact with or to depend on for the interior life of my spirit. I say this is a manlier and a higher teaching. It makes each human being for the first time spiritually free. Alone and for himself it bids him listen for the voice of God, front His judgment, sue for His mercy, and live upon His grace. What the imagination loses, the conscience gains, and spiritual manhood gains. The gain is a distinct step forward in the education of mankind—a step, therefore, which never can be permanently lost. From a system which treats men as full-grown spiritual beings and bids them live by spiritual fellowship with the Son of God, how shall we go back to a system of tutelage that guides us like children in the leading-strings of a spiritual nurse?

There is yet more to be said in the way of criticism on the Catholic theory of salvation. By placing the Christian under the care of an external society, it makes his religion to consist largely in a series of pious acts performed by rule at the bidding of a priesthood. Therefore it always runs a grave risk of degenerating into ritual, or at worst almost into magic. As the surest road to spiritual life, it asks for good Churchmanship. But one can be a good Churchman through merely conforming to outward rites. If we attend her services, perform her penances, partake of her sacraments, how can the Church refuse to pronounce us in a state of grace? Yet all these things one may do as a piece of mechanical drudgery, with no love for God or faith in Christ at all. True, the Church never professes to say that such mechanical routine will of itself save the soul. But, then, she cannot judge whether in my case it is mechanical or not. Given the outward obedience to her rules, she must pronounce me safe, for she must undertake to do her part in my salvation, since I have done mine. How can she guard against the inevitable abuse of such a system?

She never has guarded against it. Salvation by good Churchmanship has always meant in practice the encouragement on a large scale of mechanical religion. It has meant that a vast proportion of men thought it sufficient to pay their duty to the Church, and trusted in her to bear them through before God's bar. The natural outcome of the theory is, therefore, the reintroduction virtually of salvation by works, against which St. Paul combated in the Judaistic controversy of the first century. This is why the *Epistle to the Galatians* proved a weapon of infinite service in Luther's hands. This is why he made "justification by faith" the corner-stone of the Church's security. Theoretically, perhaps, the Catholic view might have been held in combination with the Evangelical way of justifying the sinner. Practically it could not. As soon as the soul is trained to look, not direct to Christ, but to Christ as represented by the Church, the temptation arises to put Churchly righteousness in the room of righteousness by faith; and Churchly righteousness means such outward conformity to Church forms as her officers can take cognizance of. A man does not need to be a new creature in order to obey to the letter the regulations of his ghostly director.

In this way the spirituality of religion, which is its very breath, comes to be imperilled. Something has come between my soul and God which undertakes to manipulate a right relationship for me with Heaven. The matter has passed to some extent out of the sphere of the hidden life of simple trust and love and fellowship with the Unseen. There is no other link of religious attachment for a soul to its Maker but the invisible link of spiritual confidence and submission. Let the Church and her priests pretend to be such a link, and at once external and indifferent actions acquire a false importance. They become the conditions of entering upon a state of grace or of remaining in it. The eye is arrested on its way to Christ and God, to rest on this nearer visible mediator. Obedience to the clergy gets confused with obedience to God. Formal actions are made to be of the essence of piety; penance, confession, and the sacraments grow into terms of salvation. And the grand canon of my text, the *Magna Charta* of a Christian's spiritual freedom, is obscured or forgotten—that the kingdom of God does not consist in external acts of religious observance, but in righteousness, peace, and joy in the Holy Ghost.

ROBBED OF ONE'S GODS.

SERMON XIV.

ROBBED OF ONE'S GODS.

"Ye have taken away my gods which I made . . . and what have I more?"—JUDG. xviii. 24.

IT would be hard indeed to imagine a more pitiable cry than this of blundering Micah when robbed of his graven image and his teraphim. He may have been a well-meaning man, but he had stumbled into very wrong doing. In a confused, anarchic, bewildering age, when every one in Israel did what was right in his own eyes, this superstitious creature had taken the precautions which he thought the best in order to secure the divine favour. He had made a private chapel of his own for Jehovah, and was seriously trying to lead a religious life, with truth and error, superstition and piety, mingled up together in a way that is the next thing to ridiculous. Suddenly, in one of the wild movements of the time, his "house of gods" was ravished by an armed band of reckless adventurers in search of a new home; and in an hour teraphim, and ephod, and self-made priest, and the whole paraphernalia of what he had called his religion, were bodily carried off before his eyes. No doubt it was a poor earthly sort of religion which stood at the mercy of a few hundred spearmen, and could be filched like a common piece of property by the passing thief. Still, it was all the man had; and if one possesses any sense of religious earnestness or the least feeling of what divine and eternal things mean, he will be more ready to pity than to smile at Micah's loss of his gods.

Unhappily this species of robbery is by no means infrequent. It comes about in a variety of ways. Although in nearly every case it indicates that something is amiss about the religion whose precious things lie so easy a prey to accident, yet the loss itself is none the less real or painful. It may even be appalling. Compared with this, one thinks, every other form of distress quite pales. Before the agony of a soul that sits alone, bereft of its spiritual treasure, its faith in the unseen and its hope for eternity, who would not stand still with a mute and shuddering compassion? Can any bereavement kill like that?

I.

The first form of such robbery I shall speak of is intellectual. There are gods of the understanding which in these days a thinking man is not unlikely to lose. The loss is in some cases serious, in others not.

We have all of us been brought up, like Micah, in the belief and fear of Jehovah, the God of revelation. Substantially that is the true faith; but it does not follow that there are no unworthy elements adhering to it in our minds, or that we hold it with entire intelligence. In every religion there are things essential and things only accessory: parts of one's creed which are vital, and parts also which are not. Betwixt these it is not always easy to discriminate. Usages, forms of worship, consecrated phrases and the like, are so many modes of conceiving or expressing divine realities. They are the body only, which encloses and reveals what is really essential in our religion. But how easily may the reverence which we entertain for God and for His eternal truth pass over to this external form and drapery of the faith! How readily may we attach to the ritual or the creed or the intellectual conceptions in which we have been trained, that heart-confidence, clinging love, and religious awe which really are due only to the Divine Saviour Himself! Especially if a man shut himself up, like Micah, in his own "house of gods," refusing for fear of the distraction of the time to look abroad and see how God is conceived of or worshipped by other men. The effect of a narrow isolated education naturally comes to be that everything about one's religion, down to its most trivial circumstances, wears in one's eyes a semi-divine sacredness. To touch a fringe is like touching the Ark. Each minute prescription of the fathers and every prepossession of our upbringing appears no less certain or important than the Divinity of Christ or the forgiveness of sins.

Such a fool's sanctuary may be rifled. Indeed, it is pretty sure to be. A belief so unintelligent that it confounds the accidents with the substance of Christianity will not be able in the light of day to hold its own. A reverence so superstitious that it worships the letter equally with the spirit must lie at the mercy of every flout cast at the letter. Some of our preconceptions on subordinate points are discovered to have but doubtful validity. The evidence for them is found weak, and their authority is blown upon. A whiff of modern thought, or a wider reading in history, or a discovery in archæology, upsets some cherished opinion, held as devoutly as we hold our hope of mercy; and in its downfall we are apt to feel as if the entire fabric were giving way. The teraphim and the images are gone. The poor soul cries aloud in its fright, "Ye have taken away my gods, and what have I left?"

Poor soul, thou hast much left thee yet. Thy gods may be pilfered from thee; but not thy God. The fringe may be torn without the Ark being captured. You have need to learn that the intellectual conceptions under which you represented to yourself eternal truth, like all other things which a man makes to himself, are liable to change. New times bring new thoughts. They demand fresh ways of understanding, and fresh formulas for expressing, the old verities. Those dear and venerable associations which from childhood wove their delicate leaves around the porch, nay, about the very altar, of your temple may have to bear the plucking of rude fingers in a day like this. But do not be afraid. God is not so easily to be stolen from His creatures; nor are His love, His mercy in the cross, His helpful Spirit of grace, trifles that can be captured and carried off by some rash speculator of the day or a novel theory in science.

The doubts which at this time are sifting, more or less, the faith of all of us, do not, in the case of the vast majority, penetrate beneath externals. Painful as they may be, there is no great cause to be alarmed, as if anything really vital were threatened. When our faith has settled itself intelligently upon what is vital, there will probably accrue no loss at all, but gain, to our religious life. But there are forms of doubt, or rather of denial, abroad, respecting which it is right to speak more seriously. One daring robber of our time, for example, does penetrate to the shrine of all belief to empty it of God. It is impossible to witness without a pang the havoc which is made in the religion of many just now by the materialism which is grown so outspoken and so confident. That science cannot discover God is true enough. No wise man would expect that it should do so. But when men in the name of science aver that they find no place for God in the universe, and that consequently He either does not exist at all, or, if He does, is undiscoverable and unknowable, they are not only unscientifically dogmatic and illogical, but they perpetrate a cruel robbery, against which it is needful to protest in the name of reason as well as of religion. The number of minds that actively embrace a philosophy of atheism is probably small. But the number of studious and candid persons among us who, while not convinced that there is no God, are yet so far shaken in their practical belief in Him and in His revelation of Himself in Christ as to draw from that belief little support or comfort, is probably pretty large. Unfortunately doubt has many degrees short of denial. In every degree it acts as an enfeebling poison on the religious life. A man may not venture to fling openly away the cherished beliefs of his youth, while yet these beliefs have ceased to be nutritive, that is to say, they retain no longer their old sustaining power. When a man has been reduced by the philosophy of agnosticism or of materialism to this point, that the God of his fathers and of his own childhood has lost all effective certainty, vitality, influence, preciousness, or helpfulness in his eyes, so that he no longer dare cling to or worship or live with the God of revelation as his God—then, say what you please, that man has suffered an incalculable loss and is spiritually beggared.

For what is there left? The void which this blank doctrine of negation leaves in the universe and in human souls, it offers us nothing to fill up. A life of goodness and valour must be lived here if we are not to sink into the swine-trough; but such a life cannot be fed upon zero or on a mark of interrogation. The nameless Something—the unknown Force—of which unbelief has to tell us, is a vain thing to still the great cry of human souls in their agony. Rifle my heart of a personal spiritual God, a Father speaking to me through Christ: how will you satisfy my hunger after righteousness? How assuage my grief for sin? How answer my spiritual ideals? How meet my craving for immortality? How supply my demand for a Being higher and nobler than myself to love, to obey, and to adore? You cannot. You have stolen from the world its God, and you leave the spirit of man a wailing wanderer in a forlorn and vacant universe, where he meets with nothing comparable to himself; a dependant creature with no one left to depend on; a child without a parent. "You have taken away my God, and what have I more?"

If the young mind that adventures itself into the modern world of inquiry is to run no risk of such a fatal loss as this, it must be because the young heart has already found God after a better fashion. The true defence lies in holding and possessing God by deeper ties of attachment than opinion, or tradition, or intellectual belief. Know God in Christ as the God of your conscience, Whose mercy in the cross has silenced the voice of guilt and awakened in you the love of holiness. Know Him as the indwelling Spirit Who inspires and answers your prayers. Know Him with the spirit as a daily Familiar—the best of Fathers and the most steadfast of Friends. Get into links of confidential fellowship with the Eternal, so that you cannot for a moment question His nearness without denying your own deepest experience. Then no intellectual difficulty can rob you of Him. The sanctuary of the intellect may be pillaged; but the sanctuary of the devout spirit, of the new life born of God, never! "He that believeth hath the witness in himself."

II.

From the gods of the understanding and how they may be lost, let me pass to the gods of the affections.

Although the heart, once rightly settled on God in Christ, cannot suffer robbery, yet our affections too often play the part of Micah over again by making to themselves gods. Something we set up in a holy place of its own, to bow ourselves down before it and serve it with our best. It is not God; but our foolish imagination decks it out in attributes like God's. We certainly expect it to do for us what only God can do. We make sacrifices for it greater than we make for God Himself. We prize it before everything else, because we dream that, so long as it is ours, nothing can quite destroy our happiness or overwhelm our spirits. Thus we begin to arrange our whole existence with this dear object for its centre, making the welfare of the whole contingent on the permanence of that one idol. I suppose we are all at one time or another tempted to do this. Some yield themselves wholly to the temptation. It is pathetic to watch the passionate fondness with which tender hearts are found clinging to such treasures, doating on them like a new-made mother over her babe. The youth may make such a divinity of his bride, the matron of her husband. As long as no adversity, like an armed band, passes that way, so long is the home counted rich and the life full. The present yields delight, and a hope vast and confident discounts its shining future.

Alas! men and women are mortal! A "wind comes

out of a cloud by night," to chill and to kill your idol. One hour of uncertainty, and it is gone : gone into the keeping of an armed foe, who turns on your tears a fierce countenance, and seems to mock you with the question, " What aileth thee ? " Aileth thee ? poor robbed heart, whose desolate cry is gone up to the heavens like a shriek : " Ye have taken away my gods, and what have I more ? "

Is that, then, a cruel robbery, I pray you ? Yes, sirs ; yes and no. *Yes :* cruel for the anguish which it works. It wrecks homes ; it shatters intellects ; it saps strong health ; it crushes young lives ; it turns unnumbered hearts to bitterness. But *no :* not cruel by reason of the justice which vindicates and the kindness which inspires it.

What is just cannot be fairly called cruel : and this is just. You and I have no right to dethrone the God Who made us in order to put a fellow-creature in His room. The ever-blessed and adorable One, Whose name be praised, merits the innermost and the chief seat in our affections. Of that seat He alone is worthy. To it He alone has claims. Are we not His spiritual children, made to be His delight and to delight in Him ? " Will a man rob God ? "[1] But ye have robbed Him—not of cattle to burn, or psalms to sing, or coins to be cast into the treasury, but of something the equivalent of which He can find nowhere else. I mean of your own reverent, grateful, and adoring regard, of your thoughtful, cheerful service, of your childlike love. Dare you accuse God of cruelly robbing you, who didst first injuriously rob Him ? This dear gift of His whom you have lost—was it not given you for a better use ? The more dear and precious it was, the more it reflected His praise Who gave it, the more ought it to have

[1] Mal. iii. 8, 9.

led your heart up in worship and thanksgiving to the Donor. It did not. It did the opposite. Given for a blessing, you make an evil of it. You it was who turned your love into a tempter, letting it steal your heart from the Highest. It was an unkindness to your beloved to do that. It was a fatal injury to yourself. You had no business to abuse a fair sweet mercy of Heaven by fabricating out of it an idol to your own undoing.

The kindest thing, therefore, which, under the circumstances, God could do for you, was to take that idol away. Do not miscall such an act by the name of cruelty. The false god was screening from you the face of the true God. Like Micah's graven image, your self-made divinity kept you from seeing truly, or loving fully, or enjoying perfectly, the Eternal Jehovah. Instead of filling the air with passionate and unavailing cries of despair, were it not better to turn back to the rifled solitary sanctuary of your own heart, and with shame-covered face sit down there, silent and repentant, before Him of Whom no enemy can deprive you? The home is not quite so desolate as you imagine, nor the life utterly empty. In the vacant seat One is come to sit to Whom all this while it did by right pertain; and if you will but let Him, He will be more to you than ten sons!

III.

To lose the idols which our own affections have made is by no means the worst form in which a loss like Micah's may be sustained. There is a spiritual form of religious bereavement which, if rarer by far, is yet harder to deal with.

I have said that God in Christ, once spiritually possessed as the soul's portion, cannot be snatched from a man by any adversary. Nevertheless, there is an experience, not infrequent with devout souls, which they are prone to call a losing of their God. Old Matthew Henry, commenting on this text, says, "Deserted souls that are lamenting after the Lord, may well admire, as Micah did, you should ask what ails them? For the tokens of God's favour are suspended, His comforts are withdrawn, and what have they more?" God forbid that I should imitate ignorant and profane persons, who, not having themselves tasted the sweetness of God's presence, can only marvel or mock at the heaviness of those who mourn His withdrawal! In sober fact, this is, of all forms of spiritual distress, the most sore. It is a distress which, if long continued for any cause, threatens the reason, and is apt to make existence itself intolerable. The intellectual loss of one's beliefs about God is bad enough; the heart's loss of loved ones whom it idolized is possibly worse; but worst of all, is that bereavement which the spiritual nature apprehends, when He Who was once its Light of life hath hidden His face away! I for one shall not marvel if one who is passing through that "valley of the shadow of death" should be reduced to cry aloud in his despair, "Ye have taken away my God, and what have I more?"

Yet, if people in this state of religious melancholy could be got to think calmly, they might see that what they have lost is not really God at all, but only certain bright and pleasant moods of their own spirit, certain states of confidence and peace which at other times they have enjoyed. These they have perhaps been taking for inseparable or indubitable pledges of the divine presence and favour; just as Micah supposed his Levite and his ephod to guarantee the blessing of Jehovah. No mistake could be greater.

Religious comfort is no infallible sign of grace. Certainly religious distress is no sign that we are fallen from grace. On the contrary, if the conscious fellowship of your Heavenly Father be so dear to your heart that the absence of it causes you continual pain; if this be the source of your pain that you apprehend God to be displeased, and in displeasure to have withdrawn Himself; then it is most certain that you are one of His children, near to His grace. Most certainly it is not Himself God has removed from you; not His favour; not His pity: it is at worst the peace that comes from being assured of His forgiveness. But with you He still is, though after a secret and unperceived fashion; hidden, but not withdrawn; unseen, not absent. Be diligent to purge yourself of whatever may justly give occasion to this trial of your faith; only recollect that it is a trial of faith, and that your appropriate duty is to wait for Him, crying after Him, and trusting Him though He slay.

What mean these various bereavings of the religious life—robberies and losses? What but this, that ours is a jealous God, and will have us inhabit no "house of gods" made with hands? Neither our orthodoxy, nor our treasures, nor our pious experiences must be suffered to stand in His room, or to intercept our religious confidence. Past all these must our faith press home, to repose nakedly upon Himself, the spiritual and eternal Jehovah. All else is shifting and insecure.

LIFE IN ABUNDANCE.

SERMON XV.

LIFE IN ABUNDANCE.

"I am come that they might have life, and that they might have it more abundantly."—St. John x. 10.

OUR Lord has here recognized that in the spiritual world, as in every other sphere of being with which we are acquainted, various degrees of vitality are to be found.

The rule obtains among all organisms on the globe that the unknown force which we call "life" exhibits itself with feebler intensity in some species than in others, and in some individuals within each species. Weak vitality in animals is marked by dulness of sensation, by a more restricted range of action, by less sensibility to pain, and by the comparative absence of intelligence. A similar diversity obtains among human beings. In many cases delicacy of constitution may be the index to a low vitality. We speak, too, of the slow understanding, the cold heart, and the feeble will. What we mean is that in such cases the life-power is scanty. On the other hand, individuals are found who seem to be all force and fire. A robust physique and a vigorous personality are far from being always combined in the same individual; but where these do combine, we recognize the conditions of exceptional power. When we meet with a man of quick perception and keen feelings, whose sympathies run swiftly in many directions, who is prompt in his decisions and so energetic in action that he can infuse into others a little of his own ardent temperament, then we all acknowledge the presence of a strong or exuberant vitality. Of him it may be said that he has abundance of life.

The striking words of my text, which Jesus dropped, as it were, by the way and left unexplained, imply that it is just the same in the higher region of Christian experience. They prepare us to find in His Church, as we do, examples of every degree of spiritual animation. Partly, this depends on natural capacity; partly on the extent to which the Holy Spirit is suffered to operate and rule within the interior life. There are lukewarm believers, and believers aflame with fervour; molluscous Christians, torpid or inert, and Christians full of faith and power. If a low type of religious vitality be unhappily prevalent in most Churches, yet we are now and then taught by illustrious exceptions of what consecration and saintliness a man is capable when he not only has in him the life of Christ, but has that life "abundantly."

Assuming such inequalities to run through every department of being from the lower to the highest, what I gather from our Lord's words is this: That God, Who delights in the presence of life, is not satisfied with any lower form of spiritual vitality where a higher can be attained; and that it has been one design of His gospel to intensify human life in all its healthy manifestations. The Son of God visited us in our far-off world, not to damp, impair, or enfeeble any of man's life-powers, but on every side to exalt them.

First of all, I think it has come true, even with reference to ordinary secular affairs, that the effect of Christianity has been, not to deaden men to the interests of this life, with its common joys and sorrows, but, on the contrary, to make their experience larger and more intense.

I know that this is not the prevalent opinion. Both the injudicious friends of Christianity and its shrewd opponents have represented it as rendering its disciples "dead to the world," in a quite different sense from that of the New Testament. Perhaps the ancient error of the ascetics is in part responsible for this current view. It is true enough that the gospel does deliver a man from exorbitant and unreasonable concern about affairs which are merely private or personal. It rids us—or it ought to rid us—of excessive longing after temporal good for its own sake; and it makes it impossible for us to indulge in extravagant regret when we forfeit temporal advantages. It teaches us to regard this world mainly as a scene of discipline. But it is a mistaken inference from this that secular pleasure and pain, gain and loss, birth and death, and whatever goes to fill up our daily round, must have lost interest or meaning for the true Christian. On the contrary, everything which happens gains in meaning and in interest by being brought, as the gospel brings it, into relationship with God and with eternity. This world itself is become a graver and a vaster place to Christians since Jesus Christ died for it. Each trifling incident—say when a sparrow falls—is seen now to be linked to the will of our Heavenly Father and woven into a plan which has man's spiritual good for its issue. Homes with their births and death-beds, their daily tables and nurseries for Christ's little ones, are infinitely more sacred spots, so near are they seen to lie to the gate of heaven. Common business rises in importance when by it you have to glorify your Saviour and serve your brother-men. Social and political problems of the hour do not claim less attention from the Christian, but more, because in them is wrapt up the welfare of that humanity for which Jesus suffered and which He calls upon us to seek and save along with Him. Christianity is so far from being a deadening influence, dulling one's concern in everything which touches the well-being of society, that it is precisely Christianity which has elevated this mean life by letting in upon it the light of eternity. It has brought into relief all its possibilities, and has made every small thing grand and every dull person noble by linking them to the destinies of our race—to the everlasting God and to the solemn cross of His dear Son.

The Christian is one who lives near to the sensorium of the universe—the heart and brain in which every sensation is felt from the remotest ends of this mighty human world: I mean the heart and brain of Him Who is "God-with-us." Through the sympathy he has with the Head of every man, the Christian's world is grown to be a very big one indeed. Shall any be weak and he not weak with them? any offended and he not burn? Christian civilization knows less and less of class interests, of isolation and indifference. Already it has knit this round globe into one, and taught every man to concern himself for mankind. The open-eyed modern Christian cares for far more interests of other people than any who ever lived before us, and cares for them far more seriously. He is in sadder earnest about greater things. He lives altogether a quicker, keener, and more multiplied life. This has Jesus done for us by His coming. The affairs of our daily existence, within the narrow circle trodden by ourselves and our neighbours, can no longer be regarded, as they used to be, with merely parochial or provincial interest, but are grown imperial now, affairs of the kingdom of God. Each man's little life, obscure or petty as it may be, is no longer like a land-locked lake, set by itself apart. It is an inlet with an open channel uniting it to the awful ocean beyond, and into it there pour day after day those mysterious tides of life which comes from the infinite heart of the Most High.

In the second place, Jesus Christ makes life to His disciple a "more abundant" thing, by conferring upon him a new kind of life, and one which has fuller pulses and a deeper, stronger vitality than merely natural or unregenerate men possess.

The experiences of Christian, that is, of regenerate life, are more profound than those of nature; because they are awakened in the reborn soul by a far grander and more powerful order of facts and relationships. Eternity is vaster than time; God mightier than the world. Men of the world are surprisingly moved sometimes by temporal losses or gains which to the eye of sober reason appear paltry. The gospel of Christ at least does not lie open to any imputation of paltriness. It sets a man into direct contact with infinite forces and with the solemn relationships of an unseen world. Its voice awakens the sense of guilt. It speaks to the soul's unquenchable thirst after God. It reveals a tremendous future of bliss or of despair. It lays us alongside the supernatural operations of God. It opens up in the cross of Christ the whole of His mighty heart. It begets in us that sacred passion for holiness, that superiority to the transient and visible, and that enthusiasm for the unseen and everlasting, which are the stuff of which heroes are made and martyrs. In short, it brings the soul within the sight and sweep of a whole world of facts which transcend this world as heaven excels the earth, and which have power to stir more absorbing desires, more overwhelming sorrows, and more rapturous joys than any that are born of time and sense.

I speak only literal truth. Judge for yourselves. Does not conversion to God add a fresh region or department to life; inspire new thoughts; quicken new emotions; suggest new motives, and place before a man new ambitions? And since by this change the horizon of his being has been enlarged to embrace Hereafter; since the fresh factor which has entered into his being to rule it, is no less a force than God Himself; since the interests for which he now labours are those of the immortal spirit with its endless destinies—it is obvious that this new life must be vastly fuller and deeper than the old one.

I do not say that it will be more noisy or demonstrative. It is with the hidden interior experiences of the soul that the gospel takes to do; with the focus of one's personal life, where one has to deal with duty, temptation, responsibility, and God. It may be that the struggles or vicissitudes of this interior life, through which as Christians we have to pass, leave less trace upon the outward demeanour than do some stormy, though shallow, passions of the animal nature. Rage, jealousy, or revenge, for example, may bluster and betray itself in voice and gesture; while the soul's conflict with ghostly adversaries, such as sin and doubt and spiritual darkness, may transpire in secret and make no sign. Yet the hidden forces are not on that account less powerful. You cannot always judge from external manifestations.

Every good student of human nature knows that the materials for the deeper tragedies of our being are to be sought within; not in turbulent animal passion, but in a soul's private wrestlings with temptation, with remorse, with avenging fate, with doubt and despair of God. In this region did even Greek tragedy find its most moving situations. Let no one suppose such hidden tragedies occur no longer. Our modern existence is less picturesque than the simpler life of the ancients, but it abounds in these underlying crises of moral experience. There is many a Christian who looks commonplace enough to you because he wears the garb of a plain trader or honest craftsman, whose inner life, could you unveil it, has been the theatre of a silent tragedy, too sacred to be dramatized, and too profound in its pathos for any sympathy to reach it save the sympathy of Christ. For it is the characteristic of the gospel that it discovers the hidden Divine in every man to whom it comes with power, and fills commonplace and otherwise vulgar natures with the energy of a divine life. This is why it has proved itself again and again to be the author of the most powerful movements in society. The strength of religious conviction working in the minds of burghers or small farmers or peasant families—say in old Rome or Gaul, in Huguenot France, in Holland, or in Puritan England—has been sufficient to create whole communities of heroes and confessors unto blood. The life of these people, otherwise undistinguished and ignoble, had been touched from above, and in the closet exercises of their faith it learned to run in deepened channels. Face to face with God in His wrath or in His grace, they found the secret of a larger life. Mightier truths than those of time kindled mightier emotions than those of sense. The homely nature dilated into grandeur, till a mob of rustic fanatics grew to be an army of saints, a host of God. Truly, when one drinks deep of the life that wells out of God through Jesus Christ, one's own life ought to become abundant.

Let me ask here: Do we know what this means? Have you ever been led to face those solemn questions of the soul, the solution of which is to be wrung out in the sweat of an inward and unwitnessed agony of prayer? Has religion entered into your life to sober and intensify every bit of it, making frivolity for ever impossible, and compelling you to live seriously? Do you recall experiences in which your peace with God, the pardon of your sin, and a solid hope for eternity were the points which pressed for settlement? Have you ever emerged from any such inward crisis with your outlook widened thenceforth, with new thoughts about your heart and a quickened pulse of moral heat throbbing through your bosom? To-day, does there lie beneath that familiar life which you lead, of diurnal toil and rest, of eating, playing, working, sleeping, another life which you dare not let go, because in it your soul privately touches God and is touched by Him; a sacred life which you keep for other eyes than ours; a life which you know to be indeed life more abundant?

There are many of us, I dare say, who can answer such questions fairly to satisfaction, who yet feel painfully conscious that any religious vitality they possess is lamentably languid and low. Have we not all reason to bemoan the feebleness of our spiritual experiences? If we possess the life of faith at all, it is certainly far from being "abundant;" for our discernment of divine truth is dim, our personal hold on it lax, our emotions towards God sickly and pale, our desires after holiness anything but keen or prevalent. In such a weak condition, we are aware that we achieve little and make no conscious headway. We feel none of the sprightliness or alacrity of spiritual health. What do we need to brace and invigorate us for our highest work for God but more abundant life?

If this be at all descriptive of your position, let me draw out of Christ's words the stinging yet encouraging lesson, that no Christian needs to be, or ought to be, content with a low degree of spiritual animation, but is bidden to seek or to admit the divine life in its fulness and abundance. In our religion, as in everything else, I believe that God would have us live strongly. The more of life we have, the better must He be pleased Who came on purpose that we might have life. He would have us respond vigorously to the tremendous truths of our holy faith. I have been seeking to remind you that everything about the gospel is large, intense, and powerful. The enormity of guilt for which Jesus died, the love which led Him to His cross, the hell from which He rescues us, the heaven of divine bliss to which He lifts us,—everything is on a vast scale, as becomes a religion which claims to sound the depths of human nature, touch its entire compass, and evoke its noblest harmonies. Therefore our response ought to be correspondingly thorough. Our joys in God, our grief for sin, our yearnings and regrets, our confidence in the Saviour and hope of His reward, our struggles for mastery over evil, our endeavours to achieve good,—ought not all these to be on a scale commensurate with the gospel? We lead a pigmy life, out of proportion to the faith we profess, if we think superficially, feel indifferently, resolve languidly, or perform little; if we can chatter with the same shallow glibness about the gloom of Calvary and the radiance of the Celestial City; if we neither tremble for dread of judgment nor burn at the words of mercy; if the deeps of our being are never stirred nor its mightiest currents set in motion by the cross of divine self-sacrifice.

I am afraid this is what too many of us do, dwarfed as we are in our spiritual development. I am bound to remind you, as well as myself, that we need not have such colourless experiences in religion, nor is it God's wish that we should. For Jesus came to shed forth on His people the Spirit of divine life in His abundance; and of that fulness may we all receive, if we will. Already we have actually God with us, about us, within us, in the plenitude of His life-power. Already, if we are Christians at all, there is a force at work upon us which is not straitened or feeble, but "able to do exceeding abundantly above all that we ask or think." Recollect how St. Paul prayed for the Christians of Ephesus, that they might know "the exceeding greatness of God's power toward us who believe." According to what standard shall we measure it? "According to that working of the strength of His might which He wrought in Christ, when He raised Him from the dead, and made Him to sit at His right hand in the heavenly places."[1] Much is heard of the gospel as a demonstration of the mercy of God, of His pitiful love for sinners. We need to be told that it no less reveals "the strength of His might;" that it is, in fact, His "power unto salvation." To be a Christian at all is to be in contact with this new and forcible activity of God the Spirit, which operates upon men's spirits to vitalize them with abundance of life—keen, high, noble, godlike life. In Him Who is the world's one life-force, as in an atmosphere,

[1] Eph. i. 17-20 (R.V.).

we spiritually "live and move and have our being." Let us open our nature wide in all its avenues. Let us beware how we obstruct His working. Let us welcome His lightest movement. Let us invite His fuller entrance and more powerful impulses. Let us yield a prompt and swift obedience to His inward touch. If we can discover the secret of daily and close communion with God in Christ, keeping ourselves in the love of God and the fellowship of the Spirit, we shall no more need to complain of a low vitality. God is to the soul like oxygen to a flame, or like air to the lungs. His fuller presence in contact with our inner being would accelerate the pulses of our blood and rouse to more vigorous action every healthy faculty of our nature. Surely it is the sorest of all our needs and the most clamant: more abundant life in the Holy Ghost!

BIBLIOGRAPHY.

[Those marked with an asterisk (*) are fugitive pieces, mostly in pamphlet form.]

* *Apostolic Times Revived.* 1859. Constable, Edinburgh.
* *Preaching Christ Crucified.* 1866. Maclaren, Edinburgh.
* *"Weep Not."* 1866. Mullen, Melbourne.
* *The Perfect Example.* 1886. Mullen, Melbourne. 1867. Maclaren, Edinburgh.

On the Written Word, etc. 1868. Strahan.
* *The First Christian Apology.* 1869. Nisbet and Co.
* *Conditions of Ministerial Success.* 1870. Nisbet and Co.
* *Words about the War.* 1870. Nisbet and Co.
* *A New Year's Pastoral.* 1870. Nisbet and Co.
* *The Office of the Eldership.* 1872. Nisbet and Co.

The Beatitudes of the Kingdom. 1872. Nisbet and Co.
The Laws of the Kingdom. 1873. Nisbet and Co.
The Relations of the Kingdom. 1874. Nisbet and Co.

The last three were collected under the title:

The Manifesto of the King: an Exposition of the Sermon on the Mount. 1881. Nisbet and Co.

From Jerusalem to Antioch. 1874. Hodder and Stoughton.

Abraham, the Friend of God. 1877. Nisbet and Co.

* *Religion the best Safeguard against the Dangers of Business Life.* 1878. Nisbet and Co.

* *The Blessed Dead.* A Funeral Sermon. 1880. Nisbet and Co.

Daily Prayers for the Household for a Month. 1881. Nisbet and Co.

Sermons. 1882. Nisbet and Co.

Commentary on Titus, in the "Popular Commentary on the New Testament." 1882. T. and T. Clark, Edinburgh.

* *Man in Relation to Nature and to God.* 1883. Publications Committee of the Presbyterian Church of England.

The Law of the Ten Words. (In the "Household Library of Exposition.") 1884. Hodder and Stoughton.

The Gospel according to St. Paul. 1888. Nisbet and Co.

www.ingramcontent.com/pod-product-compliance
Lightning Source LLC
Chambersburg PA
CBHW031815230426
43669CB00009B/1156